This book is full of the most compe̲l̲
arguably the most difficult, resistant,
world. It will challenge you to praye̲r̲
Impossible, and move you to surren̲d̲
one way or the other, to do greater e̲x̲ _____ ___ _vangelization of the Muslim
world, or just any other places resistant or hostile to the gospel.

STEPHEN BABA PANYA | President, Evangelical Church Winning All (ECWA)

I believe this book is urgently needed by God's people and others around the
world. We can no longer think this message is not relevant to us, as its one of the
most important challenges facing the body of Christ in the world today. This book
is relevant, exciting, and truthful. A must-read in the midst of so much misinforma-
tion about Muslims.

GEORGE VERWER | MBI alum, founding director of Operation Mobilization (OM)

God of the Impossible will lift your eyes to see the power of God at work in the darkest
regions of the world. You'll get a vision of God's work that strengthens your belief in
what God is doing and can do.

KARL CLAUSON | Host, Karl and Crew Mornings 90.1 FM Moody Radio; Lead
Pastor, 180 Chicago Church

God of the Impossible recounts the testimonies of former Muslims who came to faith in
Christ only then to be sent back as missionaries to share the good news of Jesus with
other Muslims. My hope and prayer as you read this book is that you will find encouragement and boldness to do the same with the people God has placed around you.

ED STETZER | Dean of the School of Mission, Ministry, and Leadership, Wheaton
College; Executive Director of the Wheaton College Billy Graham Center

God of the Impossible is a perspective-restoring reminder that God stops at nothing
"to seek and to save the lost." Your eyes will be opened to the sobering realities of
Islam, the magnificent power of the gospel, and the relentless love of God as He
pursues His treasured creation.

STEVE RICHARDSON | President, Pioneers USA

These real-life accounts will inspire your spirit and boost your faith as you discover
how the gospel is changing lives in this generation. Dr. Samuel Naaman writes not
only as a scholar but as a man with his own personal and profound story with the
Islamic world. This is must-read for those seeking to understand how God is working
in our world today.

MARK JOBE | President, Moody Bible Institute of Chicago

You will be challenged by the arduous journey these former Muslims walked, and
these stories will give the reader new hope in the power of the gospel. What sets
this book apart is that the testimonies are bookended with historical context and
practical tips to respond.

ROY OKSNEVAD | Director, Muslim Ministries EFCA

God is at work among Muslims all over the world. *God of the Impossible* is a collec-
tion of inspiring stories of dramatic conversions of Muslims of different countries
and provides practical ministerial tips and insights for all Christians everywhere to
reach Muslims effectively for Jesus Christ.

SAM GEORGE | Catalyst for Diasporas, The Lausanne Movement; editor of
Diaspora Christianities and *Desi Diaspora*

Encouraging! Informative! Convicting! From time to time, God "opens the curtains" to make us aware of what He is doing around the world. This is one of those times. You will delight in God's gracious and varied work in the lives of men and women. Highly recommended!

STEVE COFFEY | U.S. Director, Christar

I praise God for *God of the Impossible*! These stories of God in His amazing grace drawing Muslims to Jesus in the midst of suffering and persecution are riveting and encouraging. We, in the West, need this book. We need our hearts broken for these wonderful men, women, and children, and we need to see how life-changing the gospel really is!

ROB BUGH | Senior Pastor, Wheaton Bible Church

God of the Impossible opens our eyes further to the way God is on the move among Muslims all over the world. Reading these stories of transformation, hope, faith, and courage challenges us to boldly live for Jesus.

JON BURNS | President and CEO, Greater Europe Mission

God of the Impossible is a beautiful exhibit of Christ's amazing pursuit of all of us, and specifically those in the Muslim world. It details the global tapestry of faith as Christ continues to make Himself known in some of the most challenging of contexts. We should be so encouraged that our Father would go to such great lengths to pursue us!

BETH B. FROESE | Wheaton Bible Church, West Chicago, Illinois

This book is a must-read. This book can serve as a great gift to those who are engaged in Muslim ministries to encourage them and equip them even more. The stories in this book serve as a testimony that God is on the move.

ELIJAH AL FADI | President, CIRA International

God is moving mightily in unexpected places. Dr. Naaman and Rev. Fehr are on the front lines of what He is doing. This book will encourage you and help with ways you can participate in God's global mission.

JEFFREY JOHNSON | President of Tyndale House Publishers

Many books speak about Islam; this one is about the fruit of missionary work among Muslims. Reading it will encourage your heart and give you hope that God is at work among the toughest people to reach. We all need a little boost to our faith in God's ability to do what is humanly impossible.

GEORGES HOUSSNEY | President, Horizons International

When we think of complex, hard relational situations, one of them is how to interface with the Muslim world. People from an Islamic background are a cultural anathema for most Christians. For me, personally, I sensed a window being opened into a world that is culturally distant and murky. Be encouraged to start your own engagement with people God loves and seeks to redeem.

LAUREN LIBBY | International President, TWR International

God *of* the Impossible

Stories *of* hope *from* the Muslim world

Rev. Stefano Fehr
and Dr. Samuel Naaman

MOODY PUBLISHERS
CHICAGO

Edited by Mackenzie Conway
Interior Design: Brandi Davis
Cover design: Gabriel Reyes-Ordeix

All websites and phone numbers listed herein are accurate at the time of publication but may change in the future or cease to exist. The listing of website references and resources does not imply publisher endorsement of the site's entire contents. Groups and organizations are listed for informational purposes, and listing does not imply publisher endorsement of their activities.

Library of Congress Cataloging-in-Publication Data

Names: Fehr, Stefano, author. | Naaman, Samuel, author.
Title: God of the impossible : stories of hope from the Muslim world . . .
    and for your Muslim friends / Rev. Stefano Fehr & Dr. Samuel Naaman.
Description: Chicago : Moody Publishers, [2021] | Includes bibliographical
    references. | Summary: "In God of the Impossible: Stories of Hope from
    the Muslim World, you'll learn the amazing testimonies of people from a
    Muslim background coming to personal faith in Jesus Christ. In these
    riveting stories, you'll learn how to reach Muslims in your own
    community and become encouraged in your own faith by witnessing the
    power and promise of the gospel"-- Provided by publisher.
Identifiers: LCCN 2020050491 (print) | LCCN 2020050492 (ebook) | ISBN
    9780802421081 (paperback) | ISBN 9780802499189 (ebook)
Subjects: LCSH: Christian converts from Islam--Biography. | Missions to
    Muslims.
Classification: LCC BV2626.3 .F44 2021 (print) | LCC BV2626.3 (ebook) |
    DDC 248.2/4670922--dc23
LC record available at https://lccn.loc.gov/2020050491
LC ebook record available at https://lccn.loc.gov/2020050492

Originally delivered by fleets of horse-drawn wagons, the affordable paperbacks from D. L. Moody's publishing house resourced the church and served everyday people. Now, after more than 125 years of publishing and ministry, Moody Publishers' mission remains the same—even if our delivery systems have changed a bit. For more information on other books (and resources) created from a biblical perspective, go to www.moodypublishers.com or write to:

Moody Publishers
820 N. LaSalle Boulevard
Chicago, IL 60610

1 3 5 7 9 10 8 6 4 2

Printed in the United States of America

We dedicate this book firstly to the glory of God, who did the impossible when He provided a way for our sins to be forgiven and granted us eternal life. We also dedicate it to our many coworkers who tirelessly share the gospel of Jesus Christ to Muslim seekers throughout the Islamic world, and to those converts (Muslim background believers) who suffer persecution on a daily basis as they live their lives as true witnesses to their Savior Jesus Christ, and some are also martyred for their faith. You inspire us with your faith and courage.

Contents

Foreword

I read this book from beginning to end, and I recommend you do the same. Read it for *information*, for *edification*, and personal *transformation*.

Let me explain.

We who live in the West often think that Muslims simply cannot (or *will* not) come to personal faith in Christ. This book not only shares personal conversion stories, but also shows that these ten individuals represent thousands more who are coming to Christ in Muslim lands as well as right here in the United States. What makes this book so special is that it gives the cultural and national backgrounds of these spiritual journeys from Islam to Christianity. In other words, we are invited to peek behind the Muslim curtain and see that God is working even if we ourselves have not witnessed it firsthand. Read this book to be informed about what God is doing and learn how you can reach Muslims for Christ.

But also read this book for edification—this is a faith-strengthening book. It helps us understand the spiritual hunger among Muslims who are realizing that Islam can never satisfy the longing of their hearts. Reading this book makes you want to connect with your Muslim neighbors and show them that love which cannot be found anywhere in Islam can be found through Jesus and shared by His followers.

A close friend of mine who has become personally involved in the lives of Muslim refugees here in the West is now invited into their homes and is free to pray in the name of Jesus. Some Muslims are saying openly that they want to follow Jesus rather than Muhammad. We as Christians should never fear our Muslim neighbors but realize that God has created within them the same hunger that we all have to know God personally. Read the stories in this book, and you will be inspired to believe that God can indeed overcome their darkness as they come to the light of Christ.

Finally, and perhaps most importantly, read this book to be personally transformed in your heart though a determination to follow Christ no matter the cost. I felt rebuked and humbled by the suffering many Muslim believers gladly experience for Christ. In these pages, you will read the story of Abdul, who was a fake convert to Christianity in order to spy on Christians. But in a special meeting, God overcame his resistance to the gospel, bringing him to faith in Jesus Christ. He married Mary, a Christian nurse, and together had several children. Their oldest son, Solomon, had his throat slit by radical Muslims; and to make sure that he was dead, they drove knives into his heart. The sorrow of Abdul and Mary is unimaginable, but they were not deterred in their commitment to honor the Lord. At his son's funeral, God gave Abdul the strength to say to the four thousand people present, "I believe that the killers of my son are also present here today. I want to say to you: I have forgiven you. Please repent and accept the forgiveness of Jesus."

Can we read stories like this and not be ashamed of our timid and often fearful witness for Christ here in the West? We complain if we are mistreated or criticized while our brothers and sisters, converted out of Islam, stand as a rebuke to our own silence and unwillingness to take up the cross of Christ and follow it wherever it leads, namely to Golgotha. "Therefore let us go to him outside the camp and bear the reproach he endured" (Heb. 13:13 esv).

After you have read this book, your task has just begun. Think and pray about opportunities we all have to connect with Muslims. And, by the way, let us support the ministry of Call of Hope, dedicated to give hope to precious people who have been deceived by a religion that cannot keep its promises.

So, read a chapter a day and give thanks to God for those whose lives and witness speak to our hearts about the one message the world is waiting for. "For what we proclaim is not ourselves, but Jesus Christ as Lord, with ourselves as your servants for Jesus' sake. For God, who said, 'Let light shine out of darkness,' has shone in our hearts to give the light of the knowledge of the glory of God in the face of Jesus Christ" (2 Cor. 4:5–6 esv).

Read this book and you will agree that yes, there is hope that comes to us from the Muslim world.

Dr. Erwin W. Lutzer

Introduction

Until fifty years ago, hardly anyone in the West was interested in Muslims or their religion, Islam. It was largely because of the discovery of incredible oil reserves in Arabic countries and increased international terrorism that caused Islam to achieve a certain fame.

Today, Islam is no longer an exotic religion that is only thought about by scholars. With roughly three and a half million followers in the United States, it is the third largest religion after Christianity and Judaism. According to a survey by the Pew Research Center, almost half of adult Americans know a Muslim personally.[1]

Though countless news broadcasts reference Islam, most of that news is negative. This is not solely the fault of the media, as many Muslims think. Two of the most infamous dictators were Muslim: Ayatollah Khomeini and Saddam Hussein. Osama bin Laden, known only too well by the West, was a Muslim as well. Islam is a militant religion. Its founder Muhammad was a "prophet" and field commander who headed numerous raids and had his critics murdered.

The popular saying of many journalists "Bad news is the best news" is true, because bad news sells! Muslims are portrayed as brutal and threatening to us by the media; this fits the saying quite well. In this book, you will not read any "bad news" written by journalists, but you will read the amazing accounts of truly good news about which heaven is rejoicing! You will hear about Muslims who once hated Christians, but who are now our brothers and sisters in the faith. It is about people who once wanted to kill and die for the cause of Allah, who today invite their former fellow Muslims to believe in Jesus at the risk of their own lives.

In the West, there is a vast array of literature available on Islam. This writing is partly favorable toward Islam and partly critical. Yet there is one thing that most works on Islam have in common: they do not criticize Islam as a religion, but instead they criticize Muslims themselves. It is not Islamic theology that is scrutinized, but rather the crimes of the Muslims that are targeted and emphasized. It is often ignored that Muslims are really victims of their own religion. Jesus hated sin, but loved the sinner. His work of salvation, which He accomplished on the cross, also includes Muslims!

In this book, you will find the true stories of Muslims from three continents whom Jesus turned into salt and light for their countries. These are joyful, encouraging stories—"good news" that demonstrate the power of our Lord and His Word. We, the authors, have had the privilege to travel extensively and visit many of these brothers and sisters in their home countries through our ministry, Call of Hope.

I, Stefano Fehr, have been involved in mission work among Muslims for over twenty years and am part of the leadership of Call of Hope. Call of Hope was founded in 1904, and its specific

It is often ignored that Muslims are really victims of their own religion.

purpose is to spread the love of God and the good news of salvation in Jesus Christ to Muslims. My dad was the general director of Call of Hope for twenty-five years, which allowed me to grow up in a mission home and get to know many Muslim-background believers who risked their lives to tell Muslims about Jesus. We shared meals together, and they were part of our life as a family. These people of God impressed me a lot. It was always my heart's desire to serve alongside them and to be able to be part of their wonderful ministry. After my theological studies, the Lord led me and my wife back to Call of Hope. We felt that this was His calling to ministry, for which we are very thankful for. Our approach is not to send out missionaries from the West, but instead work together with locals who are missionaries in their own countries. We support them through prayer, theological training, and necessary funds. Most of our ministry workers are former Muslims themselves; you will read some of their stories in this book. Over the years, I have had the incredible joy of witnessing thousands of Muslims find peace, forgiveness, and true liberty through the encounter of God's love in Jesus Christ.

I, Samuel Naaman, am a second-generation believer from a Muslim background. My father used to be an extremist Muslim. He grew up in Kashmir, which is today part of northern India.

After the partition of India and Pakistan in 1947, my father joined the underground Muslim resistance in Kashmir against Indian rule. The fearless testimony of a young Christian girl, whom he and his fellow fighters threatened to kill, placed my father on a search for the true God. He found Christ and was baptized. Shortly after, he had to run from his own relatives who tried to kill him. He followed God's call to became an evangelist to his fellow Muslim countrymen.

Often, our family was threatened by Muslim extremists. These were the difficult circumstances under which I grew up. The worst happened on July 2, 1990, when my younger brother Obed was killed by Muslim extremists. Yet, all these difficulties have served to strengthen my personal conviction that I decided to dedicate my life to: All Muslims need to hear about the love of God in and through Jesus Christ!

Over the years working with Call of Hope, both of us have been touched by the profound love these Muslim-background believers have for their own people and the Lord. Despite ongoing persecution and hatred, they desire to reach their people with the love of Christ. These brothers and sisters in different parts of the world have given us insight into many things which we in the West can learn from Muslim converts:

1. Trust in God: Many converts find themselves in extremely difficult circumstances. They are regularly thrown out of their homes, lose their inheritance, are cut off from their own families, and often have no way to provide for themselves. Despite this, they overflow with joy, trusting God's provision, fully dependent on Him. They challenge us not to focus on our circumstances and failures, but to put our trust on the one who has all power in heaven and on earth.

2. Earnest prayer: Brother Abdul from Nigeria (see chapter 3) once told us, "I am ready to stay here in northern Nigeria and risk my life, as long as you in the West are ready to pray for me." Our brothers and sisters in the Muslim world rely on our prayers! They have experienced the power of prayer so clearly in their lives that they are convinced of the vital importance of seeking the Lord's guidance, wisdom, and protection each day.

3. Perseverance: Our friends from Muslim background don't run from problems. Most of them have had the opportunity to immigrate to the US or Western Europe, but they have chosen to remain in their own countries. One Nigerian friend has said, "The safest place on earth for me is the place where the Lord has put me."

4. Hard work: The Muslim-background believers with whom we minister are exceptionally hard working. They know the Lord is using them to spread His Word among Muslims. This is why they are willing and ready to invest their time, strength, and resources in the work the Lord has entrusted to them.

As you read the powerful stories of God's intervention and saving grace in the lives of former Muslims, we pray you will be inspired in your faith to spread God's Word to those around you as well! One day we will all worship the Lord together in eternity.

REV. STEFANO FEHR & DR. SAMUEL NAAMAN

CHAPTER 1

What a Friend We Have in Jesus

Brother Abukari
GHANA

"ONE DAY, YOU WILL BECOME A CHRISTIAN."

Abukari was jubilant. The crowd's response had unquestionably identified him as the winner of the debate at the Catholic boarding school he attended. The debate was a religious one: Islam versus Christianity. Although a Catholic school, it had a sizeable number of Muslim students. The excellent quality of education offered at the school attracted them. One of those Muslim students was Abukari.

As Abukari confidently left the debate, he ran into the headmaster of the school, a Catholic nun. He could tell that she was upset by the outcome of the debate. Sternly, she looked at him.

"You!" she said. "One day, you will become a Christian."

"No way. No way!" Abukari laughed at her, as he walked away.

THE COUNTRY OF GHANA IN WEST AFRICA

When in 1957 the West African colony called the Gold Coast declared its independence from Britain, it adopted the name "Ghana," a reference to the ancient great kingdom by the same name. Ghana was the first black African country to the south of the Sahara to gain its independence from European colonial rule. It proved to be a trendsetter. A meager ten years later, almost all African colonies had become independent from their European overlords.

This country, about the size of the state of Oregon, has around thirty million inhabitants. These belong to various tribes and language groups. At least seventy-five different languages and dialects are spoken throughout Ghana, reflecting a variety of tribes and ethnicities. The Akan people are prominent in the southern part of Ghana, while the Dagomba are an important tribe of Ghana's North. Given this great variety, it has proven beneficial for Ghana to adopt one official language: English.

Ghana is a country rich in resources. Its colonial name, the Gold Coast, already reflected this fact. Today, both gold and cocoa beans are a few of the important aspects of Ghana's economy.

MUSLIM COLONIZATION IN NORTHERN GHANA

The first Muslims to reach Ghana were most likely the Dyula people who, from the fourteenth century onward, have come in from the North (from the already Islamized parts of northern Africa). These tradesmen from present-day Mali wanted to benefit from the profitable gold trade. The resulting immigration was the key to a progressing Islamization of northern Ghana. Toward the end of the sixteenth century, the local Dagomba kingdom was dominated by Islam. Today, about 20% of Ghanaians are Muslims.[1] They continue to live mostly in the country's North.

British colonial rule facilitated the spread of the Christian message in the south of Ghana, where most of the colonial British administrative facilities were located. As a natural consequence, the coastal regions of the country were the first and primary focus of Christian missions in this British colony, while the predominantly Muslim North was neglected. However, many formerly colonized countries experienced a considerable expansion of Islamic influence during their colonial period.

REACHING GHANA'S NORTH FOR CHRIST

During the last couple of decades, the former missionary neglect of northern Ghana has been in the process of being reversed. For example, for more than thirty-five years now, our mission organization, Call of Hope, has been spreading the gospel of Jesus Christ in Ghana's Muslim North. As a result of this pioneering work, thousands of former Muslims have turned to Christ and have been baptized. Many churches have been established and tens of thousands are reached every year via radio ministry and the distribution of gospel literature.

When in 1991, a missionary of Call of Hope gave a gift of an evangelistic booklet titled "What Do You Think about Christ?" to an imam (an Islamic cleric)—he could not have imagined what the result of this simple act would be. Out of customary politeness, the imam had to accept this gift. He laid the booklet aside and, not long afterward, a visitor from a distant village came to visit the imam. While he was waiting for the imam, he noticed the booklet and picked it up. The man read some of it and then took it back with him to his own village. Being absolutely captivated by what it said about Jesus, he called the people of his village together and read the entire booklet to them! The eventual result was that many of the villagers wanted to learn more about Jesus, and receive Him as their Savior and Lord. Nearly everyone in this man's village professed their faith in Jesus! The gospel continued to spread rapidly as many churches of former Muslims were established.

ABUKARI LIVES IN TAMALE

A visitor venturing into Ghana's North can hardly bypass Tamale. It is the regional capital of that part of the country. Approaching this city of more than five hundred thousand inhabitants, the third largest in the country, one cannot help but notice its thoroughly Muslim characteristics. There are many different mosques of different sizes and shapes. The building of many of these mosques has been funded by Saudi Arabia or Iran, which are always seeking for ways to further Islam and increase their regional influence.

In the city of Tamale lives Abukari. He is a member of the Dagomba tribe, which is the dominant tribe of this part of the country.

Abukari grew up in a remote village in the north of Ghana. The name he bears is a clear indication that he is of Muslim background. In fact, to be a Dagomba is almost synonymous with being Muslim. Almost every facet of this tribe's culture and lifestyle is permeated by the religion of Islam.

Nearly everyone in this man's village professed their faith in Jesus!

Abukari's father was a man of considerable influence in his village. He had four wives, which is the maximum number of wives that Muhammad permitted a Muslim to have. The only exception to this rule was Muhammad himself! By decree of Allah, the prophet of Islam was allowed an unlimited number of wives.[2] Overall, Muhammad had thirteen wives during his lifetime.

THE BEAUTIFUL HYMN

As a child, Abukari was first sent to an Arabic-Islamic school. While there, he was indoctrinated to hate Christianity. He was taught that the Bible of the Christians was corrupted and that Christianity was a falsified religion. Later, his father decided to send him to a Catholic boarding school, where the Muslim students were allowed to practice their faith. Once a month, however, they were required to attend mass.

Even as a teenager, Abukari was already a proud and convinced Muslim. He loved debating his fellow Christian students on issues of religion. Because he was gifted as a speaker and debater, he usually prevailed in their discussions. One "victory" he achieved in a public debate held at the school was particularly special to Abukari. Even a Catholic bishop had been among the attendees.

About a month after that specific debate, all students were required to attend mass again, as usual. They were handed hymnbooks for singing. The song that was sung that day was the well-known hymn, "What a Friend We Have in Jesus."

Abukari was awestruck! Never in his life had he heard such beautiful words:

> What a Friend we have in Jesus,
>> All our sins and griefs to bear!
> What a privilege to carry
>> Everything to God in prayer!

The profound words of the hymn extended a captivating influence on Abukari's heart. Later, he explained: "As Muslims, we are a very community-oriented people. We are very sociable and always have a lot of company. But on the inside, in fact, we are very lonely. There is this profound loneliness. And now this song tells me about Someone who offers to be my friend, a real friend!"

The third verse of this hymn closes with these lines:

> Do thy friends despise, forsake thee?
>> Take it to the Lord in prayer;
> In His arms He'll take and shield thee,
>> Thou wilt find a solace there.

I absolutely must have this hymnbook, Abukari thought.

Looking in all directions, he made sure that no one was observing him. Quickly, he took the hymnbook and placed it under his jacket. Again, he glanced around; no one had noticed anything. It was important that he, the leader of the Muslim students, should not embarrass himself and "lose face" in front of the others. Then he went home and hid the book in a secret place. From time to time, he pulled it out to read the words again. What a friend we have in Jesus.

"As Muslims, we are a very community-oriented people. But on the inside, we are lonely. And now this song tells me about Someone who offers to be my friend, a real friend!"

THE KOREAN MISSIONARY

Scarcely two weeks later, as Abukari was hanging around in the neighborhood with five of his friends, they were approached by a Korean missionary. He greeted them in their mother tongue, Dagbani, and offered them two booklets. One booklet had the title, "What Must I Do to Be Saved?" and the other, "Jesus Christ in the Gospel and in the Qur'an."

Abukari was elated!

Wonderful, he thought. *I have once again found someone to argue with and show how wrong the Bible really is.*

He did not know then that these discussions concerning the Bible and the Qur'an would last a full two years.

The missionary opened up his personal library to the teenagers. "Please, take any book, and once you've read through it entirely, you may take it home, and it will be yours." That was an attractive offer. Coming from a poor background, Abukari did not possess any books of his own.

The Korean missionary did something else. He allowed the boys to play tennis on his personal tennis court. For the first time, Abukari was holding a tennis ball in hands. What an amazing feeling!

"Actually, it would be nice to have a couple of these nice tennis balls at home," the boys said to one another. So they concocted a strategy. Every week, one ball was "lost" while they were playing tennis. Later, they secretly "found" the ball and took it home. Of course, the missionary knew what was going on. But he was a man blessed with patience and wisdom and said nothing.

STUDYING SCRIPTURE

It is not easy to reach a Muslim with the message of Christ. It is not a quick thing. This is no fast-food restaurant where you can quickly serve the gospel, and everyone will be gladly and quickly satisfied. It takes time, patience, and the building of a personal relationship. And prayer, lots of prayer.

Prayer is key, as it says in James 5:16: "The prayer of a righteous person is powerful and effective."

While Abukari and the missionary were reading the Bible and the Qur'an together, they stumbled across an important verse in the Qur'an. There, it says: "And We sent none before thee, but men to whom We made revelation (i.e., previous prophets before Muhammad)—question the People of the Remembrance (i.e., the Christians and Jews), if you do not know" (16:43 and 21:7). The Qur'an contains many references to Christianity and Judaism. In fact, Islam considers them its precursors, and itself as the rightful and true heir to these religions—the last revelation of God. A comparison of the Bible and Qur'an, however, quickly shows that these religions are incompatible. Either the one or the other must be true, but both cannot be true. That is why Muslims are not allowed to read the Bible, lest they discover the truth. It is the Word of God that is most effective in leading Muslims to Christ.

Abukari and his friends showed this Qur'an verse to the imam of their village. He became enraged.

"Where did you get this? You are dangerously close to becoming Christians!"

The imam stirred up the whole village against these boys. And Abukari's father prohibited further visits to the Korean missionary.

Abukari objected. "The missionary is teaching me English!" That was an important issue for his father, so he relented. "Well, in that case, okay, you may go."

Thus, the visits continued and also the faith discussions.

ABUKARI FINDS HIS TRUEST FRIEND

It did not take much longer after that. For two years Abukari had studied the Bible. He had come to realize that it is the true Word of God. He had also come to realize that Jesus is Lord, and that He offers to be his personal Savior.

At sixteen years of age, he trusted Jesus with his life. Finally, he had found this very personal friend. What a great joy!

Outwardly, however, this was the beginning of a lot of troubles for him. In becoming a Christian, Abukari had brought shame to his father's house, and even to the whole village.

Abukari's father told him: "You are either a Muslim and can enjoy all the privileges of being a son in my home; or you are a Christian and you have to leave my home and look after yourself." His mother cried a lot, but she as well insisted: "Please leave our home."

So, Abukari was chased from his parents' home. No money, no clothes, no food.

The local church stepped in to help. They paid his school fees and provided food for him to eat.

After his graduation from high school, Abukari went to Tamale, where he found a job as an assistant in a mission organization's office. It was a distribution center for Christian and evangelistic literature. When he saw the literature that was printed and distributed from there, he was astonished. Those were the very booklets that the Korean missionary had given to him that had played such a vital role on his journey to finding Christ! He had, in fact, started working in the literature center of Call of Hope in Ghana.

Today, Brother Abukari is in charge of this literature center and is coordinating the ministry work of Call of Hope in Ghana. Thousands of Muslims in northern Ghana, especially young people, are reached from this ministry with gospel literature and in various other ways every year. The light of the love of God that reached his heart is now reaching others. Abukari has followed in the footsteps of the Korean missionary who reached out to him. He is now reaching out to many others.

One final note: After Abukari had become a Christian, he went back to the Catholic nun at his school and confessed to her that he had stolen the hymnbook from the church. He wanted to give it back. This time around, she was the one laughing. "You may keep it," she said. "You have now become a Christian."

HOW CAN I REACH MUSLIMS FOR CHRIST?

This story shows us an important principle for winning Muslims to Christ: The power of relationship! Reaching out to and building up a relationship of appreciation and friendship with a Muslim neighbor or colleague is a powerful evangelistic tool. Abukari came to Christ in no small part because of the love and patience of a missionary. Abukari and his friends were welcomed into the missionary's everyday life. They played tennis and shared stories and meals over a period of time. The missionary was a good listener and encourager. He respected their family background, culture, and beliefs. Yet all along he found creative ways to bring up the gospel in many instances and conversations.

Relationship and hospitality allow Muslims to see God working in our lives. Listening to their stories, learning of their heritage, and their family and background are the first steps for us in the West. It may take some time, but lays a solid foundation of trust and mutual respect that opens doors for the gospel. It often is a prerequisite for sharing the love of Jesus and the message of the Bible.

CHAPTER 2

One Sentence That Pierced the Heart

Brother Ishak
TURKEY

THE ADULTERESS

With intense concentration, Ishak listened to the unfamiliar voice over the radio.

It was the early 1980s. The war between Iraq and Iran was raging at full height. At the time, Ishak was in his early twenties and was a student in the Faculty of Islam in Ankara, Turkey. That evening, he had visited some of his fellow students from Iraq. Some of them had relatives who were battling on the frontlines. They decided to search the air waves for an Iraqi radio station that could bring them news from the war zone.

Instead, they stumbled upon a Christian radio broadcast. The radio host was speaking about the story of an adulteress who was caught in the act of transgression and brought to Jesus. Jesus was asked to pass judgment over her.

As a future imam, Ishak knew full well what had to happen to an adulterous woman according to Islamic law. Down to the last detail, the sharia law (the civil and criminal law derived from the Qur'an and the Hadith) prescribes how the stoning of such an adulteress has to be performed: She must be buried in the ground up to her stomach. Also, she has to wear a thick shirt, so that those stoning her will not sin by looking at the exposed naked skin of a woman.

According to Islamic law, the case was crystal clear. The sharia court would pronounce the death sentence. But what would Jesus say?

TURKEY—A BIBLICAL PAST, AN ISLAMIC PRESENT

The Republic of Turkey is situated right on the border of Asia and Europe. Istanbul, its largest city, is the only major metropolis in the world to straddle two continents! The Anatolian peninsula—which is mainland Turkey—is the westernmost protrusion of Asia, the largest continent in the world.

Ancient times saw powerful Hittite kingdoms in this region. Their influence stretched right down to the Holy Land, as their frequent mention in the Old Testament also shows. Later, in the time of the New Testament, this became gospel heartland. In fact, this region, also called Asia Minor, is second in importance only to the Holy Land to the history of early Christianity. It was here, in the city of Antioch that the followers of Jesus Christ were first called "Christians" (Acts 11:26). The apostle Paul traveled extensively throughout Asia Minor on behalf of the gospel and founded many churches in different cities. Located in Asia Minor are also the seven churches which Jesus Christ Himself addressed directly in the Revelation of John. We can read these letters in Revelation chapters 2 and 3.

When in the fifth century Turkic tribes from Central Asia started their westward expansion toward Europe, present-day Turkey was still staunchly Christian. It was the center of the orthodox Christian Byzantine Empire. From the ninth century on, these Turkic tribes converted to Islam. The warring ethos that is inherent to Islam, called jihad or holy war, suited them well. It did not take long before the whole Middle East and even large parts of southeast Europe were under the control of these excellent warriors. The Byzantine Empire (the last bastion of the Roman Empire) lasted a thousand years and fell in 1453 when the Turkish emperor Sultan Mehmed II conquered the city of Constantinople. Henceforth, the House of Osman would rule here, and their Ottoman Empire stretched from Algiers in the West to Baghdad in the East, from Belgrade in the North to Mecca in the South.

After a rule that lasted many centuries, the remains of this vast Turkish-Islamic Empire crumbled in the aftermath of World War I. Modern-day Turkey was founded in 1923 as a secular republic.

Today, very little of Turkey's original Christian heritage remains. In spite of being one of the more secular Muslim countries, 99.8 percent of its population claims formal allegiance to Islam.[1]

In the 1980s, there were only about fifty Turkish believers in Christ from Muslim background in the country. These Muslim-background believers were even outnumbered by the number of Christian missionaries who were working in Turkey! To these few believers, however, would soon be added another convert: Ishak.

A SMALL TURKISH VILLAGE
ON THE SHORES OF THE BLACK SEA

Ishak was born in a small village bordering the Black Sea in north-east Turkey. His parents and grandparents lived together in the same big, old house. His parents were Muslims in name only. They never performed salat, the five-times-a-day ritualistic Islamic prayer. The only person at home who did follow the Islamic prayer was Ishak's grandmother. Only twice a year did his grandfather visit the mosque: Eid al-Fitr (the Feast of Breaking the Fast, after the end of the fasting month of Ramadan) and Eid al-Adha (the Feast of the Sacrifice), two of the most important festivals of the year.

When Ishak attended primary school, the school offered no Islamic religious education. Back then, Turkey was even more secular than it is today. To fill in this gap, his grandfather bought him a subscription of a magazine about the life of the prophet Muhammad. Once a month the magazine was delivered to their house. This was the first form of Islamic teaching that Ishak had ever received.

Learning about Muhammad was a mixed experience for him. On the one hand, he was glad that the prophet Muhammad was able to defeat his enemies. However, he thought that the way in which he handled his enemies was ruthless.

"Would it not have been better if our prophet had not killed his enemies?" he asked his grandmother one day.

His grandmother was shocked to hear such a question. "My child, don't think about such things. We can't understand his ways. Muhammad is a prophet and always acts according to the will of Allah."

RELIGIOUS EDUCATION AND COMMUNIST FRIENDS

By the time Ishak entered high school, the Turkish government had made Islamic religious education part of the school curriculum. His religion class teacher was a nice man who wanted his students to become proud Muslim citizens. He emphasized the greatness of Islam saying, "Only Muslims are allowed to perform their prayers everywhere. Christians can only pray to God in a church."

Ishak was sad to hear this proclamation. His neighbor was an Armenian Christian, who knew how to make the best local vinegar! He was unhappy to hear that this man could not pray, since there was no church in their town. It was only later he came to know that this was untrue and that the beautiful town mosque had formerly been an Armenian church.

The Islam teacher also told them the Muslim view of the history of the Bible. Apparently, Christians had falsified the true gospel of Isa (the Arabic name for Jesus in the Qur'an), and hundreds of different gospels had been written! To resolve this untenable situation, the church fathers had supposedly put all these different gospels on a large table, then shaken the table, and all gospel versions had fallen off the table, except the four still read by Christians today!

Ishak was far from convinced that Islam was a great religion. However, of one thing he was sure: that Islam was far superior to Christianity.

In his later high school years, Ishak became involved with the local communists, largely because the communist rejection of Islam appealed to him. He started spending most of his time in the youth club of the Communist Party and barely attended school anymore. He considered it his duty to learn by heart the biography of the Soviet leader Brezhnev. In spite of this lack of school attendance, Ishak's grades were outstanding. The influence that his local communist friends had at school was very "helpful" in that regard.

ADMITTED TO THE FACULTY OF ISLAM

After completing high school—with outstanding grades—he wanted to go to university to study. To do this, Ishak had to participate in a countrywide university entrance exam. He also had to list his top-five study course choices. His preferred choices were either geography or linguistics. On the advice of a friend, he half jokingly listed "Islamic Theology" as his fifth study choice. This friend said: "We need communist imams to destroy this backward desert religion!"

The entrance exam went horribly. His lack of a proper high school education, thanks to his communist "friends," now fully manifested itself. Ishak fully expected that he had failed the test.

However, one month later the mailman arrived at his house, waving a card in his hand. "Congratulations, boy, you have made it. You have been admitted to university. You will become the first Islamic theologian from our village!" On the postcard it was printed in large letters: ADMITTED TO THE STUDIES OF ISLAMIC THEOLOGY.

Ishak was shocked. He, who neither believed in Allah nor liked the prophet of Islam, Muhammad, who had never been in a mosque and who himself had never before performed the Islamic prayer—he should study Islamic theology and become an imam? He could not even read or write Arabic!

His communist friends mocked him. His grandfather also complained, "Only sons of peasants study Islamic theology!" His parents, however, were glad that he had been admitted to university at all. Ishak decided to give it a try and moved to Ankara, the capital of Turkey.

ANKARA—BAGHDAD—AND INCREASING DOUBTS

The first hurdle that needed to be taken was to learn Arabic. By chance he got to know an Iraqi Jew who was living in Ankara. He was an elderly man in need of assistance, and in exchange for Ishak taking care of him, he taught Ishak Arabic. This Iraqi Jew was an excellent teacher. At times, Ishak was reading hundreds of pages of Arabic literature every day to his sight-impaired teacher. After only one year, Ishak in his knowledge of Arabic had already surpassed some of his university teachers!

Ishak now also read many of the most important works of Islamic theology in Arabic. This did not fail to have a profound effect on him. Slowly, he became more and more convinced of the truth of Islam. Soon he voluntarily started performing the Islamic ritual prayer. His attire also changed, and he started dressing like a pious Muslim.

Ishak still kept up outward appearances and continued to pray publicly. Deep inside, however, he had already started to abandon Islam.

Due to his excellent study progress, Ishak received a scholarship from the prestigious Islamic Faculty at the University of Baghdad in Iraq at the end of his second semester in Ankara. During his two years of study there, his class lectures included critical questions and discussions about Islam and its history. This study started to plant seeds of doubt about this religion in Ishak's mind.

In the midst of this uncertainty, Ishak experienced an event that would further his hesitations about Islam. One day, he witnessed a terrorist attack by Islamists on an Iraqi army convoy in the streets of Baghdad. Seeing torn bodies lying in the street, this horrifying incident, performed in the name of Allah, shook Ishak and made him even more skeptical about Islam.

When after two years he returned to Turkey, his faith was shaken. Ishak still kept up outward appearances and continued to pray publicly. Deep inside, however, he had already started to abandon Islam. And even while he still cursed the "infidels in Europe and America" as well as the "Zionist government of Israel," on the inside he already felt differently about these things.

THE RADIO BROADCAST

During this period, he was visiting with some fellow Iraqi students who were studying in Turkey. It was the time of the war between Iraq and Iran, and his Iraqi friends had relatives who were soldiers with the Iraqi army. They were searching for an Iraqi radio station in order to find out the latest news concerning the ongoing hostilities.

The radio reception was particularly bad that evening. Suddenly, they came across a radio broadcast of unknown origin. In very clear and well-pronounced Arabic, a voice was preaching on the story about the woman who was caught in the act of adultery and then brought to Jesus (see John 8:1–11). The religious leaders expected Jesus to pass judgment on the adulteress according to Jewish religious law.

This story from the gospel of John immediately caught Ishak's attention. From his excellent knowledge of the Qur'an, he did not know about such an incident in the life of the prophet Isa. Also, the Hadith, the Sayings of Muhammad, did not contain such a story. He realized that this must be a story from the Bible.

JESUS VERSUS MUHAMMAD

As a prospective imam, Ishak also knew about an "Islamic version" of this story, where an adulteress was brought to the prophet Muhammad so that he should pass the proper judgment on her according to Islamic law. Since this adulteress was found pregnant, Muhammad first sent her home. Then later, after she had given birth to her child, she was stoned. Islam knows of no mercy for the sinner. It does not differentiate between the sin and the sinner.

These thoughts and images where flashing through Ishak's mind while he and his friends were following the broadcast. Suddenly, the voice from the radio detailed the response of Jesus to the women's accusers:

"Let any one of you who is without sin be the first to throw a stone at her." (John 8:7)

Ishak was stunned! It was as if the words of this one sentence had pierced right through to the core of his being. Walking home later that night, he could not shake the feeling that everyone walking past him was able to see exactly what sins and crimes he had already committed in his life and what evil thoughts he harbored in his mind.

The Holy Spirit had found a powerful entrance into his life through just one sentence from Scripture.

SEARCHING FOR A BIBLE

He now wanted to find a Bible and read for himself the story of Jesus and the adulteress. But this was easier said than done. He visited all the book shops in Ankara. No Bible was to be found. Finally, he found a very old Arabic Bible in a secondhand bookshop. The price: five thousand dollars. Sad and angry, he gave up his search.

A couple of days later, a surprising thing happened. As he was approaching the door of the Islamic Faculty where he studied, Ishak noticed a group of Western-looking men standing close to the entrance.

"Who are these men?" he asked the doorman.

"These are Christian pastors and theologians from Europe. They are participating in a conference of Islamic-Christian dialogue."

The Holy Spirit had found a powerful entrance into his life through just one sentence from Scripture.

This was exciting news! These were not just ordinary Christians; these were theologians and pastors. Surely, it would be possible to obtain a Bible from one of them.

Cautiously, Ishak approached the group. "Who of you is a pastor?" he asked.

A man introduced himself to him as a pastor from Belgium. He even could speak Arabic. Quietly, Ishak asked him whether he was able to give him a Bible in his mother tongue, Turkish, or otherwise in Arabic. This pastor's answer took him completely by surprise.

"Why do you need a Bible, my friend?" he asked. "You have your Qur'an. In it you find everything that you will also find in the Bible. Both books have the same origin. We are all children of Abraham."

Ishak at first just stared at him. Then he grew anxious. Maybe this man was no pastor at all, maybe he was an undercover Muslim and would pass on the news to the secret police that someone had asked him for a Bible! Ishak's first encounter with a Christian pastor from the West in search for a Bible turned out to be rather traumatic.

"THANK YOU FOR SUFFERING FOR MY SINS."

Where could he get a Bible? Ishak remembered the Christian radio station where he had heard the sermon about the adulteress. It took him some time to find it again on the radio. He noted their address and sent them a letter. Less than two weeks later, he received a parcel with evangelistic literature. This was the start of his journey in his search for the truth. Later, he also received the Gospel of John.

During his semester break, Ishak read through the Gospel of John more than twenty times in just three weeks. One night, after having read the last chapter of John again, he knelt down and for the first time in his life prayed to Jesus Christ.

"Thank You for suffering so much for my sins. Thank You for dying this cruel death on the cross for me. Thank You for patiently searching for me, me who was lost, for such a long time."

Following his conversion, Ishak was visited by missionaries from Call of Hope. This was the beginning of a connection that continues on today. While he was yet in his last semester of Islamic studies in Ankara, he was already translating evangelistic literature for the mission into Turkish. Later, he himself started working with Call of Hope.

In the last thirty years, Brother Ishak has traveled extensively all across the globe, and especially to Muslim countries. Drawing from his vast insight into Muslim theology, he has in countless seminars spoken to Christian missionaries and evangelists laboring in the Islamic world about how to best reach Muslims for Christ.

But it all started with just one sentence from the Bible out of the mouth of Jesus.

HOW CAN I REACH MUSLIMS FOR CHRIST?

The story of Brother Ishak illustrates the power of the Word of God and the power of even a single verse of the Bible. All it took was one sentence from Scripture to turn Ishak, the student of Islam, into an outright seeker of Christ. This example is repeated over and over in the world of Islam. On a daily basis, missionaries in Islamic countries can witness to the truth of Hebrews 4:12: "For the word of God is alive and active." Another convert, G. M. Naaman, who is author Samuel's own father, also said, "The sooner you bring a Muslim to reading the Word of God, the better it is, as the Word itself will convict and call a person to the truth."

The Bible's availability in written and electronic form provides a person the chance to hear God's voice in his or her heart language. We would like to encourage you to use the powerful tool of the Word of God in reaching out to your Muslim friends and neighbors. Possible ways to do this may be, for example, the gift of a calendar with printed Bible verses at year end or writing a birthday card and including a verse from Scripture.

CHAPTER 3

A "Faker" Becomes
a True "Follower"

Brother Abdul
NIGERIA

"WHY DID HE HAVE TO DIE . . . ?"

The atmosphere in the living room of the small apartment of Brother Abdul was tense. It was not the heat outside, or the irritating humming of countless mosquitoes, or the power outage that had already lasted for two weeks. The silence was saturated with a profound sense of sadness. Only the noise of the power generator could be heard.

On the sideboard, next to the wall, stood a picture on display of the family's eldest son, Solomon, with a small bouquet of flowers next to it. A cord stretched from wall to wall with condolence cards hanging from it.

The trembling voice of Brother Abdul broke the silence.

"Why did he have to die, why was he slaughtered like a goat ...? He died all by himself, Lord. Why ... ? Didn't You promise to always protect us and our children ...? Am I not laboring on Your behalf in spreading the gospel to Muslims?"

Just two weeks earlier, an Islamist hit squad had killed Solomon right on the university campus in Abuja, Nigeria, where he was studying.

THE REALITY OF THE PERSECUTED CHURCH

Christians living in the West often do not realize how blessed they are to enjoy the religious freedoms enshrined in their country's constitutions. For many of our fellow brothers and sisters living all over the world, this is not the case. In fact, the persecution of believers in Christ has never been more intense than it is today. According to Open Doors, around 260 million Christians in the world today are threatened by serious forms of persecution because of their faith.[1] This is the suffering church. It is suffering together with Christ and for the sake of His name, until His glorious return.

Nigeria is one of those countries where millions of Christians are currently suffering for their faith. If one were able to hear all the voices of the martyrs joined into a choir of suffering praise to God, the Nigerian section would be featured prominently, singing beautiful African melodies of praise to God, a sobering and yet magnificent sound.

THE APOSTLE JOHN SEES THE SUFFERING CHURCH

The sixth chapter of the book of Revelation in Scripture gives a voice to these all-too-often silently suffering members of the body of Christ.

The apostle John recounts,

> When he opened the fifth seal, I saw under the altar the souls of those who had been slain because of the word of God and the testimony they had maintained. They called out in a loud voice, "How long, Sovereign Lord, holy and true, until you judge the inhabitants of the earth and avenge our blood?" Then each of them was given a white robe, and they were told to wait a little longer, until the full number of their fellow servants, their brothers and sisters, were killed just as they had been. (Rev. 6:9–11)

This passage gives us insight into the attention God gives His suffering church and those who are martyred for believing in Jesus—He listens to their cries. God has allowed their suffering to happen, but it is not in vain, and He Himself will one day comfort them. This is also clearly communicated when the story is picked up again in the next chapter of Revelation.

> After this I looked, and there before me was a great multitude that no one could count, from every nation, tribe, people and language, standing before the throne and before the Lamb. . . . Then one of the elders asked me, "These in white robes—who are they, and where did they come from?"

I answered, "Sir, you know."

And he said, "These are they who have come out of the great tribulation."...

"they are before the throne of God
and serve him day and night in his temple;
and he who sits on the throne will shelter them with his
presence....

'And God will wipe away every tear from their eyes.'"
(Rev. 7:9, 13–15, 17)

NIGERIA—A COUNTRY DIVIDED IN TWO

With more than 200 million inhabitants, Nigeria is by far the most populous country on the African continent. About twice the size of California, it is divided into a predominantly Islamic North and a Christian South. There are historic reasons for this geographic religious division within the country. From the fifteenth century on, Islam became established in northern Nigeria, particularly among the Hausa and Fulani tribes. In the early nineteenth century, the Fulani declared a jihad (holy war), which led to the establishment of a caliphate, consisting of several semiautonomous emirates.

British colonial rule began in southern Nigeria in the second half of the nineteenth century. By 1903, the northern emirates had also been conquered, and the country joined together as one. Christian missionary activities flourished in the South but were severely restricted in the North.

In 1960, Nigeria became independent. The following decades were often marked by turmoil and violence, including civil war.

The year 1999 saw the transition to a democratic government from military rule. Starting that same year, the twelve northern Nigerian states began to introduce the sharia as state law, which is the Islamic law derived from the Qur'an and the Hadith.

THE BOKO HARAM AND ISLAMIC TERROR

For some radical Islamists, this was not enough. They wanted to completely eradicate all traces of Christianity and Western influence from the country's North. Only Islam and its practices should be present in the country, they believed. The terror organization Boko Haram was established to pursue this goal. The word "boko" means "fake" and refers to all that is Western, particularly Western education. The Arabic word "haram" means "forbidden." Thus, boko haram means: Western influence and education is forbidden. This motto has become a horror and nightmare for many people in northern Nigeria: Christian villages and churches have been attacked and burned, tens of thousands of Christians have been killed, and millions have been displaced.

Unfortunately, in spite of some government efforts against Boko Haram, terror has not subsided in recent years and new terror groups including the so-called Fulani militia have emerged.

These are the difficult circumstances under which Brother Abdul labors on behalf of the gospel. He is spreading the love of God to Muslim believers, wherever and whenever possible. But before he found Christ, Brother Abdul himself was persecuting Christian believers!

ABDUL IS TERRIFIED OF HELL

Abdul was very devout to his Muslim faith. At a young age, he studied the Qur'an for several years and had been recognized as a mullah—an Islamic scholar. Diligently, he followed all the teachings of Islam. He was very much aware of the fact that in order to—hopefully—qualify for entry into paradise, he would have to perform scores of good deeds. Abdul hoped that by weight of his many good deeds, his time in hell would be as mild and as short as possible, before—hopefully—Allah would allow him to enter heaven.

Yet he was unable to find inner peace. On the contrary, he was terrified of death. His greatest fear was related to that extremely narrow bridge, which Muslims believe they must cross after death in order to reach paradise. Abdul was afraid that he would be among those who fall from the bridge into hell and suffer torture.

But before he found Christ, Brother Abdul himself was persecuting Christian believers!

He even performed the hajj (pilgrimage) to Mecca. But his inner fear and torture only increased.

COVERT OPERATIONS

Because Abdul was in the grip of this fear, he decided to participate in the persecution of Christians. He was convinced that this would dramatically increase his chances of avoiding hell and entering into paradise, so he became part of a Muslim organization.

So, one day Abdul entered a church service and took a seat

at the very back. He listened and observed carefully the way in which Christians spoke and how they behaved. Week after week, he returned. Then he reported to his Muslim elders what he had observed and what he had heard during the church announcements. This allowed the Muslims to disrupt activities planned by the church. During that time, Abdul also secretly participated in the torching of many churches.

A FAKE BELIEVER

As time went by, Abdul decided to professionalize his anti-Christian enterprise. He went to see the pastor of the church that he had been regularly attending for some time by then.

"I would like to become a Christian," he declared.

"That is wonderful news!"

The pastor was very happy to hear this; he really liked Abdul. He took Abdul in and for six months, Abdul received Bible and baptism instruction. After those six months, he was baptized and received full membership in the church. Yet, he continued his covert operations against the church. Nobody had a suspicion of what he was doing. He was even promoted and became leader of the church's youth group and occasionally was allowed to preach.

One day, Abdul learned about a large shipment of Bibles destined for northern Nigeria. It was expected to arrive in Lagos, the large port city on the southern coast of Nigeria. These Bibles were a donation for churches and believers in the North.

Upon learning this, he activated a team of his young militant Muslim friends.

"Guys, we have a thing to pull off here!"

Off they went, southward to Lagos. Abdul was well connected to a couple of Muslim politicians and government officials. This helped them locate the container where the Bibles were stored. Abdul and his friends then proceeded to dump tens of thousands of Bibles into the sea. All the Bibles that believers in northern Nigeria were eagerly expecting were destroyed!

WHY ARE CHRISTIANS SO HAPPY?

Abdul was convinced that this action had once again scored him bonus points with Allah and had increased his chances to enter paradise. And still, his inner unrest remained. In fact, the more he increased his "good deeds" against Christians, the more his inner panic grew!

During this time, he continued to attend the weekly church services and pass on inside information to the Muslim organization. He couldn't help but notice that the Christians seemed to be much happier than he himself ever was. Christian believers never gave an indication to have a fear of hell. Somehow, they possessed the certainty that they would be able to enter heaven directly.

Such a conviction by itself seemed blasphemous to Abdul. A Muslim believer is not allowed to be certain about his or her salvation. Only Allah knows and at his own will decides who will be saved and who will go to hell.

A CONFERENCE BECOMES THE TURNING POINT

For six full years, Abdul worked undercover in the church against the church.

One day some of the church youth invited him to attend a large conference at the church together with them.

"Will I be the speaker at this conference?" he inquired. No, that was not the case. His church friends explained to him that an elderly pastor had been scheduled as the conference speaker.

Abdul was not pleased. He coveted the honor of being the speaker. In the end, he agreed to go along with his friends.

There were about two thousand participants in this three-day conference. Already during the first two days, the old pastor's preaching had made an impression on Abdul. Then came the last service of the conference. The topic of the sermon was: "Who is the only true God?"

The pastor cited from the story of Elijah in Scripture: "How long will you waver between two opinions? If the LORD is God, follow him; but if Baal is God, follow him" (1 Kings 18:21).

Abdul felt cornered. It was as if the preacher were speaking only to him. *How does this guy know me and my situation?* he thought.

The preacher now directly looked at him. "How long will you waver? If you want to be a Christian, then really be a Christian!"

Abdul's head started to spin. *Did one of my friends tell him about me? Maybe John?*

The preacher continued, "You think maybe that nobody knows about you? God knows you!"

Yes, I know that God knows me, Abdul thought. *Apparently you know me also. This has been going on for six years now already. I really need help to get out of this mess.*

"I would like to help you," sounded the voice of the old pastor from the pulpit. "But you have to do something. Please stand up, so that I can pray for you."

Abdul resisted. Never could I stand up in front of everyone! Yet it was as if a supernatural power from heaven dragged him to his feet. He stood up. Then he peeked around to see how many others had stood up also. Of the two thousand in attendance, he was the only one standing!

"Come here to the front and let me pray for you," the pastor said.

Kneeling down, Abdul surrendered his life to Jesus. That conference became the turning point in his life.

A BEAUTIFUL NURSE NAMED MARY

Persecution was the immediate consequence of his conversion to Christ. His former Muslim friends and even some of his relatives wanted to kill Abdul for leaving the Islamic faith. In order to protect him, the church arranged for Abdul to stay with an old pastor in another village.

This friendly elderly minister took him in like a son. Out of respect, Abdul always called him "pastor"—he didn't even know or ask for his name!

"I like you. God likes you. I really like you." The pastor patted Abdul on his shoulder. "I'm praying for you, that God will give you a wonderful, beautiful wife."

One day, Abdul went on a youth outreach to another city. They did hospital visitations and ministered to the sick. In the hospital, he saw a beautiful nurse. They talked a little together. She had such a beautiful smile.

"Would you like to marry me?" Abdul asked her. Mary didn't answer that question but just smiled beautifully at him. That was all the encouragement Abdul needed. Surely she was in love with him!

As quickly as possible, he returned to the pastor with which he was staying.

"Pastor, I have found my wife!"

"Praise the Lord!" the pastor said. "I have been praying for this to happen. Can you tell me the girl's name? Do you know the name of her father?"

Abdul didn't know. He had not asked. It would be necessary to know these things to initiate the marriage negotiations. At the next opportunity, he rushed back to the hospital and searched for the beautiful nurse. He found her. "Please, I need to know your name and the name of your father!"

He went back home to his pastor.

"I now can tell you—her name is Mary; her father's name is Mamman!"

The pastor threw his hands up in the air. Abdul knew that signal. In his country it meant: I'm in big trouble.

"I have been praying for you for a wife. And now the Lord has put me to the test. That nurse Mary is my daughter!"

The marriage arrangements proved convenient. Pastor Mamman was the father who paid the bride price, and he was the father who received the bride price. God blessed their marriage with four children. Together, they devoted their lives to winning Muslims for Christ in Nigeria.

PAYING THE ULTIMATE PRICE

Mary and Abdul have been faithfully serving the Lord together in Islamic northern Nigeria for many years now. Their heart's desire is that many more Muslims may still come out of the darkness of Islam and into the wonderful light of the Lord Jesus Christ. As they are laboring under these difficult circumstances, they both have come to know what it means to suffer for the sake of Christ. Once, an angry Muslim mob gathered outside their house, threatening to kill them. They escaped by the skin of their teeth. Their house was burned down. Some of their Christian neighbors were not as lucky and were killed.

A couple of years later, Abdul and Mary took a young Muslim convert whose life was in danger into their home. His relatives demanded that he return to Islam. The Muslim community warned Brother Abdul not to shelter this young man anymore. Otherwise they would take revenge.

Brother Abdul felt that it was his duty to help this young believer. Had not he as well received shelter and protection when he was a young believer in Christ?

At the time, Brother Abdul's oldest son, Solomon, was studying at the university in Nigeria's capital, Abuja. One day, a Muslim killer squad with motorcycles drove right onto the university campus with one intent, revenge. Spotting Solomon, the squad leader cried out: "Kill him!" Then they cut his throat. To make sure that he really was dead, they stuck their knives into Solomon's heart.

"WE WILL HONOR GOD."

It was Brother Abdul's sister-in-law who discovered the body of Solomon at the morgue of the hospital where she was working. It was such a shock that for several minutes she screamed and cried. The parents and the whole family were devastated.

It was a difficult time for the family. They were mourning and crying. But in the midst of these circumstances, Brother Abdul said, "Even if they kill all our four children—every loss of a child will draw us closer to the Lord, until one day we will be with Him."

And Abdul's wife, Sister Mary, said: "If this was God's will for us—if He has allowed this to happen—we will still honor Him."

Four thousand people attended Solomon's funeral, including the state governor. Some of Brother Abdul's relatives, who had refused to see him for over forty years because he had become a Christian, also attended. When the governor saw the masses of people, he ordered for sacks of rice, sugar, and oil to be delivered in order to provide food for everyone. The young Muslim convert, who had been taken care of by Brother Abdul, also came to the funeral, in spite of the security concerns. "I have to come; I have to be there. He died in my place," he said.

God gave Brother Abdul the strength to say at the funeral, "I believe that the killers of my son are also present here today. I want to say to you: I have forgiven you! Please repent and accept also the forgiveness of Jesus."

God used the opportunity for His glory. "The blood of Christians is seed," said church father Tertullian, meaning that the blood of those martyred is not wasted but, in God's mysterious but wonderful way, brings about new life in the church.

> **"I believe that the killers of my son are also present here today. I want to say to you: I have forgiven you! Please repent and accept also the forgiveness of Jesus."**

Brother Abdul said, "The devil wants to throw us down into despair. But we know that through all this, God is pulling us even closer to Himself. It may happen that more of our children are taken away from us. But with the Lord, whom we serve, we will always come out on top in the end. Psalm 43:5 teaches us to say: 'Why, my soul, are you downcast? Why so disturbed within me? Put your hope in God, for I will yet praise him, my Savior and my God.'"

HOW CAN WE HELP THOSE WHO FACE PERSECUTION?

Unfortunately, the history of Christianity is not a blank sheet when it comes to the issue of tolerance for those of other faiths. It includes the Crusades and other atrocities committed in the name of Christ over the course of the last twenty centuries. However, these wrongs that have been committed by certain individuals, churches, or countries are completely incompatible with the teachings of Jesus Christ as we read them in New Testament (see Matt. 5:38–44; Rom. 12:17–21).

We do not find these same principles of love and tolerance for those of a different faith or one's enemies in Islam. Jihad, the holy war, is a method used to help the spread of Islam. Historically, most of Islam's geographical advances have come through military conquest. The prophet Muhammad himself fought multiple wars for the cause of Islam. A mere eighty years after the death of Muhammad in 632 AD, Muslim armies had conquered a vast swath of land that stretched from Spain and over all of northern Africa through the Middle East right up to the borders of India and China. Most of the conquered indigenous populations were forcibly Islamized over the centuries that followed.

Islam recognizes the use of force as a legitimate means for the defense of Islam, for example, against a person who has apostatized from the Muslim faith. Therefore, extreme persecution frequently accompanies a Muslim who leaves Islam to follow Jesus. In fact, Islamic sharia law calls for the killing of anyone who deserts Islam. This is the reason why those who kill a Muslim-background Christian face little to no consequences for their actions. Even in the West, we see those who come to Christ pay a heavy price. Will we stand alongside them? Provide shelter when it is needed, and speak on their behalf?

Where, then, is justice? It is left in the hands of the only Righteous Judge. This is illustrated over and over by Christians living in the Muslim world.

Brother Abdul continues to serve in the northern Nigerian Sharia states, where many Christians are facing the atrocities of Boko Haram on a daily basis. From our brothers and sisters who are living in the world of Islam, we can learn how to respond in the right way to persecution. They take seriously the words of Jesus, "I tell you, love your enemies and pray for those who persecute you" (Matt. 5:44).

CHAPTER 4

"Jesus Loves Me—
a Woman!"

Sister Elmira
LEBANON and SYRIA

A REFUGEE HOT SPOT IN THE BEKAA

Miserable is the life of the refugee. After the civil war in Syria in 2011 unleashed its destructive forces, millions of Syrians fled the war zones. Hundreds of thousands of them took refuge in Lebanon. The Bekaa Valley in mountainous eastern Lebanon became a refugee hot spot. This is where the Syrian Muslim refugees set up their tents. Many came with nothing more than the clothes on their back. No carpets, mattresses, or blankets were inside their tents. Some did not survive the harsh winter conditions in the Bekaa Valley. Yet one woman managed not only to survive here, but to find the true Life of the world. God used the harsh conditions of a Lebanese refugee camp to bring Sister Elmira to Himself.

LEBANON—BEAUTY AND ASHES

Lebanon is a small country in the Middle East surrounded by the Mediterranean Sea to the west, Israel to the south, and Syria to the east and north. Lebanon has sometimes been referred to as the "Switzerland of the Middle East." This is due in part to its banking policies, but even more so due to its natural beauty. This is a country where you could go skiing in the morning on a beautiful mountain slope and in the afternoon descend to the coast and take a swim in the ocean. The highest peak of the Mount Lebanon mountain range, which traverses the country from north to south, is the Qurnat as Sawda' at more than ten thousand feet, making it one of the highest mountains in the whole Middle East.

Lebanon features prominently in the Bible and is mentioned more than seventy times in Scripture. King Solomon famously imported cedar trees from Lebanon to build his magnificent temple. Cedar is still Lebanon's national tree and adorns the country's flag. Famous Mount Hermon in southern Lebanon is associated in the Bible with beauty and nature's praise to God. As it says in Psalm 133:1, 3:

> How good and pleasant it is
>   when God's people live together in unity! . . .
> It is as if the dew of Hermon
>   were falling on Mount Zion.
> For there the LORD bestows his blessing,
>   even life forevermore.

Sadly, Lebanon has witnessed anything but peace and unity in recent decades.

From 1975 until 1990, a bloody and cruel civil war was waged between Lebanon's then majority Christian population and its Muslim population factions. Tens of thousands were killed, while hundreds of thousands more became refugees and fled the country. Formerly the only majority-Christian Arab country in the world, Lebanon now has a majority Muslim population. A fragile peace exists between the three major factions of the country, each accounting for about a third of the population: Shiite Muslim, Sunni Muslim, and Maronite Catholic.

The country's situation is further complicated by the presence of the many refugees, up to two million Palestinians and Syrians. That is a huge number, especially if one considers that only around four and half million native Lebanese citizens are living in the country.

A MINISTRY AMONG SYRIAN REFUGEES

Brother John, a missionary with Call of Hope, has been reaching out to Syrian refugees in the Bekaa Valley with the love of Christ through practical and spiritual aid. He and his team visit refugee camps and distribute food, other aid items, and gospel literature.

The fact that John is reaching out to Muslims is a miracle in itself. Actually, like many Christian Arabs in Lebanon, he used to hate Muslims due to the cruelty he experienced at their hands during the civil war.

Sometimes refugees ask him why he, a Christian, is helping them, Muslims. Brother John is always more than willing to explain:

"The only reason for this is JESUS! I used to hate you, the Muslims. I even wanted to kill as many of you as possible, because during the civil war in Lebanon, Muslims bombed and killed several of my relatives.

"Hate had filled my life, and I held guns and wanted to kill Muslims. But then I found Jesus—and He completely changed my life! He forgave my sins; He helped me to forgive and He even gave me His love for you—the Muslims!

"And this same Jesus can also change your life!"

ELMIRA COMES TO THE CHURCH

Love is the most powerful force for change in the world. It cannot be faked.

Recognizing true love is the reason why many refugees in the camps opened their tents and their hearts to Brother John and allowed him to enter and share with them from the true message of divine love.

The news spread that there was an open heart and open hand for the refugees. By the hundreds, the refugees were now coming to John's church to directly request aid. Many of those who came attended the worship services and attentively listened to the pastor's teachings.

The Word of God never returns empty. More than four hundred of these Muslim refugees gave their hearts and lives to Christ in the last several years. Thus, in a short period of time, God has called into existence a church of Muslim-background believers in the Bekaa Valley through the ministry of Brother John.

One of those Muslims who came to this church was Sister Elmira.

Originally from Damascus, Elmira and her son had fled to the Bekaa Valley in Lebanon due to the civil war in Syria. She came to Brother John's church in search of life-sustaining aid. She also stayed for the church service and listened to the sermon. And she came back and listened some more.

After a while, she approached Brother John.

"I had heard the rumors how at your church even Syrians and Muslims are welcome and are accepted. That's why I came to you."

Elmira then went on to tell Brother John her personal story.

MARRIED AT THE AGE OF TEN

Elmira came from a family of nine children and grew up in the urban context of Damascus. Elmira was the youngest of the six girls in the family. Her parents were Sunni Muslims, and Elmira's father had arranged the marriages for her older sisters when they were around twelve or thirteen years old.

It is not uncommon in observant Muslim circles to marry off young girls. This practice is based on Muslim sharia law and draws its legitimacy from the fact that, according to Islamic tradition, the prophet Muhammad married one of his wives, Aisha, at the age of six and entered into marital relations with her when she was nine. Following the prophet's example, the sharia permits marriage for girls nine years and older.

When Elmira was nine years old, her father entered into negotiations with an middle-aged man who wanted to marry her. One of Elmira's older brothers objected.

"My sister is only a child; she is too young to get married!"

"It's no problem that she is still a child; I can raise her at my home," the man said.

One day, as Elmira was playing with her baby doll, her mother entered the room. "Get up, you must put on your clothes; I am going to take you on a trip."

"I cannot go now, Mommy. I am busy feeding my doll—it is not good to leave her hungry!" Elmira had put out some small plates with rice and yogurt and was taking good care of her doll.

"You can feed her when you come back. Come along now already."

LIFE IS HELL ON EARTH

Elmira did not know that her marriage had already been arranged and registered. She was only ten years old. She was taken to the house of her new parents-in-law where her future husband waited for her.

"Listen, you must stay here. You cannot come home with us," her father told her.

No explanation was given to her. Elmira saw that her father received money from this strange man, whom she didn't know, but who she now had to stay with. Maybe her parents had sold her to him?

After her family had gone home, she was left sitting all by herself next to the strange man.

"I am your husband," he said.

Elmira started to weep uncontrollably.

She had never gone outside her parents' house alone, she did not go to school, she did not have any friends—her doll and her toys were her friends. And now, all of a sudden, she was in an unfamiliar place with a strange man sitting next to her who told her he was her husband.

Elmira tried to wriggle away and keep the man from touching her. The man hit her strongly.

"I am your husband," he again said.

Elmira did not know what he meant by that. She cried and wept.

Two days later her husband bound her with a rope and raped her.

He also did other cruel things to her. Sometimes, as a punishment, he took her into the bathroom and poured ice-cold water over her. Once, he broke both her wrists. He also had the habit of rubbing out his cigarette butts on her bare skin.

"Why do you do this to me?" Elmira pleaded with him.

"I enjoy hearing the sound the cigarette makes as it is extinguished on your skin," her husband cruelly replied. Elmira's body is still full of marks and scars today.

Due to this abuse, Elmira developed psychological problems. On visits back home, she received little sympathy from her parents. They were afraid Elmira's husband might divorce her.

When Elmira had turned eleven, her body entered puberty. Not long afterward she became pregnant. The doctor warned her husband that at this tender age, she could very well die while giving birth. He did not care.

Miraculously, Elmira survived and gave birth to a son and then later to another son.

COMING TO LEBANON

In order to provide for her two children, Elmira's husband requested that she start working. This took place just a couple of weeks before the outbreak of the civil war in Syria in 2011. In the beginning stages of that war, her husband was killed.

While her older son remained behind in Syria, Elmira, together with her younger son, made her way to Lebanon as a refugee.

There, she eventually remarried: Aahed, a Shiite Muslim became her new husband. Aahed proved to be a tender and kind husband. He truly loved her. What a difference from her first marriage experience!

At the same time, she started coming to Brother John's church and was overwhelmed by the kind reception and the love she received there.

Sitting through many services and listening to the sermons, she came to understand the reason for the love and acceptance that was on clear display among the people.

"I have been coming to your meetings for a while now already, and have listened to your teachings.

"At first, I could not understand the reason for your love toward Syrians and Muslims—but now I do. The reason for your love is Jesus! Jesus loves us and died for us on the cross.

"And what is more, I now also know and understand that Jesus loves even me and respects me—even as a woman! I want to have this Jesus in my life!"

"HONEY, WHY SHOULD I KILL YOU? I LOVE YOU!"

Brother John and his wife had many in-depth conversations with Elmira about the truths of Scripture and what it means to become a Christian. In the end, Elmira accepted Jesus as her personal Lord and Savior. She was overjoyed!

For a while, Elmira kept her new faith in Christ secret from her Muslim husband, Aahed. She feared his reaction in case he found out that she had left Islam. She knew, however, that she could not hide the facts from him indefinitely.

"At first, I could not understand the reason for your love toward Syrians and Muslims— but now I do. The reason for your love is Jesus!"

It took her a couple of months until she had gathered enough courage to tell him the truth. One day she went to talk to him about the matter.

"Listen, Aahed, I have to tell you something. The church where I've been going to and have received aid from—those are truly good people. And I have listened to their teachings about Jesus, and I must tell you, I have also come to believe in Jesus—I am a Christian today.

"Now, I know that this will be shocking news for you, and maybe you will want to kill me because you think I have betrayed Islam, but I am willing and ready to die for Jesus!"

Elmira anxiously watched her husband's facial expression as she finished speaking. How would he react? To her surprise and great relief, Aahed seemed neither shocked nor angry. He smiled at her. "Honey, why should I kill you? I love you!" he said.

"Moreover, I have noticed a positive change in the last couple of months. You have even become a better wife to me. I have wondered what could be the reason for this change. Now I know—it is your new faith in Jesus. I myself would like to learn more about this Jesus!"

"BERINE" MEANS "WHITE"

Nothing could have given Elmira greater joy and satisfaction than to introduce her husband to Jesus, the one who had accepted her, loved her, and saved her.

She invited him to attend church with her. After the service, he met with Brother John, and they entered into conversation. A couple of times, they met together at Brother John's office, studying God's Word together and discussing faith-related questions.

Not long afterward, Aahed was ready to accept Jesus as well.

He told his wife, "I now share the same conviction as you. I know Jesus is the Truth and He is Lord. And I love Jesus, because He is a lord of peace. He is the Prince of Peace."

It was an occasion of joy and celebration when both of them received their baptism on the same day. Moreover, it was also Sister Elmira's birthday. She had specifically requested this.

"God has been so good to me. From now on, whenever I celebrate my birthday, I will be reminded of the goodness of God, and that Jesus loves me!"

Not long afterward, the Lord blessed this couple with the

birth of a beautiful baby girl. She was named Berine. They asked Pastor John to dedicate their girl to the Lord during a church service in front of the assembled congregation.

"What is the meaning of 'Berine'?" John asked the couple, as they were standing in front of the church.

"'Berine' means 'white,'" they replied. Elmira explained. "My life was in complete and utter misery, pain, and darkness in the past. Now Jesus has saved me, and He has brought me light, love, peace, and healing."

"Our lives used to be in the darkness of Islam," Aahed added. "But now together with the Lord Jesus, they have become white, just like the snow. That is why we named our daughter Berine."

> **"Our lives used to be in the darkness of Islam. But now together with the Lord Jesus, they have become white, just like the snow."**

WHAT POSITION DO WOMEN HOLD IN ISLAM?

No other people group suffer under the law of Islam more than Muslim women. In a few years, it is likely that the number of Muslims worldwide will reach two billion. This means there are roughly one billion Muslim women—close to one billion people whose most basic human rights are often trampled on in the name of Allah and his prophet, Muhammad.

Within the Islamic worldview, a woman has less value than a man. The Qur'an does not view a woman as an autonomous being, and also not as a being of equal worth with a man, but as someone under guardianship, who should be guided and controlled.[1] A woman's testimony in Islamic court is only worth half the testimony of a male person.[2] The same goes in the case of an inheritance—women as a general rule receive less.[3] And, according to sharia law, a Muslim husband can divorce his wife by simply saying a specific phrase.[4]

Christianity holds a completely different view. The Bible states that both men and women are created in the image of God (Gen. 1:27). God Himself made Eve, the first woman, from a rib taken from Adam's side. Thereafter, God presented her to him. Thus, God took a part from the man to make for him a companion, a "perfect fit," to be his counterpart (see Gen. 2:18–24). In making Eve, God's plan was not to create man's "double," but to have them complement one another. From a biblical point of view, women are not devalued or seen as a flaw in creation.

The first man and woman were originally created sinless, but through their disobedience they fell from their perfect fellowship with God. But because God so loved the world, God's Son Jesus Christ died for all our sins, and now the relationship with God of both women and men can be restored.

Many Muslim women today are struck by the fact that Jesus loves them and that in God's eyes they are equally important as men: "There is neither Jew nor Gentile, neither slave nor free, nor is there male and female, for you are all one in Christ Jesus" (Gal. 3:28). If we as Christians approach Muslim women with respect and dignity, they will sense the difference. Often, they become very open to learning more about the love of Jesus and may even dedicate their lives to Him.

CHAPTER 5

The Lady Who Wanted to Clean the Church

Sister Fatima
LEBANON and SYRIA

SURVIVING AS REFUGEES IN LEBANON

Fatima was standing in the midst of the remains of her family's once beautiful home. Like much of the rest of their hometown, the heavy bombing by Assad's government forces had laid it to rubble. The town of Zabadani was almost completely destroyed.

Zabadani had been the first town under the control of anti-government rebel forces at the start of the civil war. This beautiful tourist town near the Lebanese border went on to see many heavy battles between rebel and government forces in the years that followed. Many of the inhabitants were killed and thousands fled, mostly to neighboring Lebanon.

Among those who fled to Lebanon were Fatima and her family.

Fatima's family used to be financially secure. Her husband was the owner of an aluminum factory, and they and their four children lived in a three-thousand square foot house. Fatima, a graphic designer, was professionally involved in the designing and making of couture for TV actors.

The civil war completely destroyed their lives in Syria. The company was decimated as well as their home. They lost most of their belongings and financial means. Moreover, Fatima's husband was injured in the war and became disabled.

They fled to Lebanon and settled in the Bekaa Valley, where they were able to rent a small room. For a short while, they received minor financial support through the UNHCR, the United Nations refugee agency. Eventually, this also came to an end. There were just too many refugees in need of support who had come to Lebanon.

The family possessed absolutely nothing. On the garbage dump, they found some old mattresses and dirty blankets to use in their home. Because of his injuries, Fatima's husband was unable to work and sustain their family. How could one survive under these circumstances?

THE CIVIL WAR IN SYRIA

According to some estimates, the civil war in Syria, which started in 2011, led to the killing of more than four hundred thousand people, many of them civilians.[1] Additionally, more than six million Syrians fled their home country, while an additional six million people were internally displaced in what is recorded as one of the largest humanitarian crises in recent world history.

Civil unrest started with protests against president Bashar al-Assad. This was the period that has since has been dubbed the "Arab Spring." Protest movements blossomed all over the Middle East and North Africa. By the end of 2011, the conflict in Syria had escalated to a full-blown civil war. Part of the government forces changed sides and fought with the citizens. However, if those opposing Assad had hoped to be successful as quickly as other protest movements in Tunisia and Egypt, they were to be disappointed. President Assad clung to power and was prepared to use any means necessary to maintain it. The long-drawn struggle came at a steep price, a price paid by the people of Syria in blood and destruction.

Other regional and world powers jumped into the fray for humanitarian reasons or because of their personal power interests. The Assad regime was backed by Iran and Russia. The Iranian-linked Hezbollah fighters from neighboring Lebanon assisted Assad's army on the ground. Russia helped the Syrian government troops with air power. Western and Arab governments mostly declared their support for the rebel forces. This support remained somewhat timid, however, likely due to the presence of radical Islamist terrorist groups in rebel-held territory, like the al-Nusra Front.

Islamist presence took on alarming proportions when the terror group ISIS (Islamic State in Iraq and Syria) seized control of large parts of eastern Syria in the Euphrates Valley. Eventually,

ISIS was defeated by Turkey-backed rebel forces in the country's northwest, US-backed Kurdish fighters in the northeast, and Syrian government forces in the rest of the country.

Arguably the greatest tragedy of the ongoing crisis in Syria is the countless people who were killed or displaced, like Fatima and her family, who fled to the Bekaa Valley. Who would take care of them?

A CHURCH CENTER
FOR MUSLIM-BACKGROUND BELIEVERS

In 2008, Brother John started a new spiritual project in the Bekaa Valley. It became his goal and passion to start a church of Muslim-background believers in that area (see also the previous chapter). A small room was rented for the first meetings.

Yet, Brother John had a greater vision. In faith, he started with the construction of a building that would be suitable for the needs of a small church center: a meeting room able to hold up to one hundred worshipers, a room for children's services, and other basic necessities. The funds for the construction of the building were provided by mission friends in the United States and Germany.

God's great adversary, Satan, apparently was not too happy with these developments. The construction company contracted to build the church center deceived them and used a cement of very poor quality for the construction of the building. The whole edifice had to be torn down and rebuilt from scratch. At last, in 2011, the building process came to completion. This was just a couple of weeks before the start of the civil war in neighboring Syria!

Syrian refugees started to pour across the border into Lebanon by the thousands, and they lacked the basic necessities of life.

Brother John's work was cut out for him: reaching out to these destitute people with a helping hand and a loving heart. The word started to spread, and by the hundreds and thousands, the Syrian refugees came and were glad to receive aid and listen to the Word of God in the refugee camps and at Brother John's church.

FATIMA WANTS TO CLEAN THE CHURCH

A refugee woman told Fatima about "this Lebanese Christian man" who was giving out aid to Syrian refugees at his church. Thus, she ventured to go to the church of Brother John. There she received food for her family.

She also attended the church service that day. The Word of God spoke to her heart. She came back not only to receive more food, but also because of a hunger for God had been awakened in her soul.

One day, Fatima stayed behind after the church service to speak with Brother John and his wife.

"I would like to clean the meeting room after the service."

"Don't feel like you have to pay us back for the aid you are receiving—it is for free!" the couple replied with joy.

"I know, but I still would like to clean the room," Fatima said.

So they allowed her to stay behind after the Sunday service and clean the room.

Soon Brother John and his wife discovered the real reason

She came back not only to receive further food, but also because of a hunger for God had been awakened in her soul.

behind Fatima's offer to clean the church room: she loved the privacy it offered, when all the other church visitors had already left, to ask them questions concerning the Christian faith. Fatima had long conversations with Brother John's wife. Everything was so new and different from what she had been taught in Islam.

THE "JESUS PRINCIPLE"

At one church meeting, Brother John was preaching on the parable of the Good Samaritan told by Jesus as it is recorded in Luke 10. He expanded on three different motivations or principles that are discernable in that story.

The first principle on display is the satanic principle: What is yours is mine. The robbers assault, rob, and badly injure a person traveling from Jerusalem to Jericho. It is naked and violent egotism!

Second, there is the human principle on display: What is mine is mine and what is yours is yours. In other words, your problems are none of my business! If each person just looks after themselves, everyone will be looked after! In this story, the priest and the Levite travel past the injured man and look the other way.

Third, we witness another principle in this story, the Jesus principle: What is mine is also yours. It is the principle of "love thy neighbor as thyself." My neighbor and their needs matter to me. I share what I have with you. The good samaritan made the dire situation of the injured man his own business. Likewise,

Jesus also came to earth to "serve, and to give his life as a ransom for many" (Mark 10:45).

Fatima listened to Brother John's message intently.

What he was preaching there in front of the congregation was not mere talk. She had seen this "Jesus principle" at work in Brother John's own life and ministry and in his outreach to Syrian refugees on numerous occasions. She herself and her family had been beneficiaries of it.

At the end of his sermon, Brother John offered an invitation to personally receive Jesus Christ. That day Fatima accepted Jesus as her personal Lord and Savior!

SUFFERING FOR THE SAKE OF CHRIST

After her conversion to Christ, Fatima continued in fellowship at Brother John's church. She quickly grew in the Lord and in her understanding of Scripture. She was so full of joy that she started to share her faith in Christ at home and with her friends and relatives.

This witness for Christ drew an immediate and strong backlash.

She showed Brother John some of the threatening messages she had received on her phone:

"We know that you have left Islam, and we know that you are going to a church. One day we will come and kill you," one message read.

Undeterred, Fatima did not relent from following Jesus and sharing His good news.

A couple of months later, Fatima's aunt appeared at their

home. She had brought with her a stick and started beating Fatima strongly on her head, her arms, and her legs.

"If you do not stop going to a church, I will tell your uncle, and he will come and kill you!" her aunt screamed.

Fatima told her husband, Nasser, about this incident, and she was grateful that he stepped in and went to see her aunt, telling her, "Stop disturbing my wife, or else I will notify the police!"

This incident did not stop Fatima from continuing to attend the church meetings. Unfortunately, her aunt also did not refrain from harassing her. She arranged for a sheik, an Islamic scholar, to visit Fatima.

"You are a smart woman," the scholar addressed her. "Why did you leave Islam?"

"You say that I am a smart woman? Well, that is exactly why I believed in Christ! It is the best thing I could do," Fatima replied.

The sheik got angry. "Tell me, how can we make you reconsider your decision and come back to Islam? Is there anything you need? Do you need money? A car?"

"You are offering me things that are temporal and will soon be gone in exchange for something that is eternal and cannot be taken from me."

Exasperated, the sheik gave up trying to convince her. "She has an evil Christian spirit."

AN ASSASSINATION ATTEMPT

One afternoon some time later, Fatima was on her way to the weekly women's meeting at the church. The trip was a couple of miles, and her five-year-old son was walking with her.

Suddenly, two men on motorcycles rode up from behind. They jumped off their bikes and started to hit her with an iron rod and stones.

Her young son started screaming and crying, "Mommy, mommy!"

The two men continued to furiously beat her until Fatima fell to the ground, unconscious. She was bleeding heavily from a large wound. The men thought that she was dead and fled the scene on their motorcycles.

A passerby found Fatima there, lying unconscious on the ground with her son standing next to her, screaming. He took her to the hospital, and the doctors examined her and found that she had suffered a fractured skull.

"You are not allowed to walk for the next nine months," the doctor said to her once she awoke. "You are not allowed to expose your head to rain, cold, or sunshine, and you have to stay inside and spend most of the time lying on your back."

UNDETERRED

Brother John and his wife came to visit Fatima at her small home.

"Please, I need a whole stack of copies of the New Testament and tracts so that I can pass them on to those who come to visit me," she told Brother John as she was lying on a thin mattress on the floor. "My Muslim relatives and friends need to continue to hear the good news of salvation in Jesus Christ!"

Brother John had never before seen anyone evangelizing and

passing out gospel literature as eagerly as Sister Fatima in those nine months while she was lying there on her mattress, injured and hurting because of her love for Jesus.

She also said, "Whatever happens to me, I will never ever leave my Lord Jesus. His joy is still with me. I forgive those who tried to kill me. They really do not know the truth. I pray for them, so that they can find the Savior, the One who loves them, and find the same peace that I have."

"I THANK GOD FOR THE WAR IN SYRIA!"

The months passed and Sister Fatima's recovery made good progress. Eventually, she was able to get up from her sickbed. Some negative health effects of the beating, however, were permanent. Periodically, her body is still plagued with tremors.

Now she could go to church again. What a joy to see all her spiritual brothers and sisters, most of whom, just like herself, were from a Muslim background, and had been touched by the incomparable love of God. Together, they worshiped and praised the God who truly cared for them and had given them eternal life through faith in Jesus Christ.

Sister Fatima became part of the church staff and took care of the children's Sunday school service.

One day, she said to Brother John, "I thank God for the war in Syria!"

"Excuse me, what?" exclaimed Brother John. "You lost everything you had in Syria, your home, your possessions, some of your family members . . . How can you say that you thank God for the war in Syria?"

"It is true," Fatima replied. "I thank God for the war in Syria. Because without it, I would not have come to Lebanon, and I would not have found Christ's love and eternal life! And to me, that means more than anything else!"

I forgive those who tried to kill me. They really do not know the truth. I pray for them, so that they can find the Savior.

HOW CAN I REACH MUSLIMS FOR CHRIST?

Brother John's life and ministry reflected this unconditional love of God, and the genuine love he exhibited touched Fatima and was instrumental in bringing her to faith in Jesus Christ. For many Muslims, it is a life-changing experience to witness the true love of God in the lives of believers.

The god of Islam, Allah, is different from the God of the Bible. The Qur'an pictures Allah as almighty but distant. Humans cannot reason with him.[2] He may lead a person in the right way or lead him astray, as he pleases.[3] He may show favor toward the righteous, if it pleases him to do so, but he despises the sinners.[4] Although he is often given the title, "the merciful," his mercy only applies to the righteous.[5] Muslims do not call God "Father"!

By contrast, we believe that "God is love" (1 John 4:8). This statement by the apostle John is central to the Christian understanding of God. God loves all people, even sinners, regardless of their personal attitude toward Him. "He causes his sun to rise on the evil and the good, and sends rain on the righteous and the unrighteous" (Matt. 5:45). The God of the Bible is loving, kind, and desires to have intimate fellowship with His children, who He invites to call Him "Abba!" (Dad). Because our God is a God of love, the command to love God and your neighbor as yourself is at the center of the Christian life.

If we want to reach Muslims for Christ, the first thing we need to do is to ask the Lord to give us genuine love for Muslims. Without sincere love, which only God can give us, our attempts to reach Muslims will remain fruitless.

CHAPTER 6

A Young Moroccan's Journey to Christ

Brother Karim
MOROCCO

THE HOUSE CHURCH MEETING

The small group of eleven Muslim-background believers from four different families had inconspicuously entered the house in a suburb of Casablanca, where they gathered in the basement for Sunday church service. They made sure all the windows and blinds were closed before they proceeded to a time of muted singing and praise to God. Today was a special day: Brother Karim had come and would share from the Word of God!

NORTHERN AFRICA WAS A HEARTLAND
OF CHRISTIANITY

The Kingdom of Morocco lays claim to the oldest ruling dynasty in the Islamic world, the Alaoutie dynasty. King Mohammed VI, who ascended the throne in 1999, unites the highest political and religious powers of the country. The royal house claims descent from the prophet Muhammad. The country's motto, visibly displayed in many public places, is the "trinity" of Allah, Country, and King. The overwhelming majority of Moroccans are Muslims of Sunni affiliation. Officially, there does not exist an indigenous Moroccan Christian church, and native Moroccans are prohibited by law from entering the beautiful church edifices in the country that stem from the Spanish and French colonial period.

Long ago, the religious landscape in Morocco looked much different—as in all of northern Africa. In fact, the now completely Islamized countries of North Africa—Egypt, Libya, Algeria, Tunisia, and Morocco—used to be a heartland of Christianity in the first centuries AD. Numerous prominent theologians of the early church period hail from here, among them Tertullian, Origen, Athanasius, and Augustine. After periods of harsh persecution under various Roman emperors, there arose a large and powerful Christian church in northern Africa sparked by Constantine the Great's conversion and leadership (306–337 AD). In the fifth century, in what is today Algeria, Tunisia, and Morocco, there were more than six hundred bishops charged with overseeing church affairs.

THE MUSLIM INVASION

Then came the Islamic conquest of northern Africa. In 640 AD, only eight years after the death of the prophet Muhammad, Egypt was invaded by Arab armies. The attack was made from the Sinai Peninsula. In three short years, Egypt was subdued and Muslim rule was established. The pressure and terror exerted by the invaders on the native population as well as the heavy taxation of non-Muslims led to a mass conversion to Islam.

After the conquest of Egypt, the jihadist armies turned their eyes farther westward. There lay more countries and peoples to conquer, more churches to plunder, and more territory to subjugate to the rule of Allah.

The farther west the Muslim armies pushed, the fiercer the resistance they met. The regions of Algeria and Morocco were inhabited by the Berber people who were known for their military skills and ferociousness. While powerful Egypt had fallen in just three years, it took the Arab armies more than fifty years and many hard-fought—and some lost—battles to conquer all of present-day Morocco.

As in all the places they conquered, the new Arab rulers pursued a policy of strict Islamization and Arabization. The local Berber population was forbidden to write or publish in their native dialect and was forced to learn Arabic. This policy lasted in Morocco up to the twentieth century. By the thirteenth century, a complete Islamization had been achieved in Morocco. No Christian believers remained in this once-Christian country. For many centuries, Morocco remained completely closed to the gospel.

On paper, this is still the case. By Moroccan law, it is a crime to evangelize a Moroccan native or cause them to doubt the teachings of Islam. It was estimated that in the 1960s, there were no more than twenty Moroccan believers from a Muslim background. The last couple of decades, however, have witnessed the birth and growth of an underground church in Morocco. Today there is a network of believers who are meeting in small underground house churches all over Morocco. The body of Christ is growing every year in this lovely African country. One of the pioneers of this little-noticed movement of Christ in Morocco over the past decades is Brother Karim.

BORN IN THE ATLAS MOUNTAINS

From southwest Morocco through northern Algeria up to northwestern Tunisia are the spectacular and beautiful Atlas Mountains. They form a natural border to the vast Sahara Desert lying to the south. The higher mountain peaks of the Atlas are usually covered with snow. Brother Karim was born here in one of the picturesque Berber villages, which are scattered throughout the mountains of southwestern Morocco.

Karim's parents, of course, were Muslim. The family was divided in two: The father's side of the family had a tradition of tradesmanship, while on the mother's side the emphasis was on religion: Karim's grandfather and his uncles were Islamic clerics, faqihs (Islamic jurists), and sheiks (Islamic scholars). Politically his family was divided also. Half the family favored the socialist left and the other half was supportive of the moderate Islamists.

The family spoke Tashelhit at home, one of the major Berber languages.

At the age of five, Karim was sent to the local madrasa, the religious Islamic school adjoined to the village mosque. The task here was to learn Arabic, memorize the Qur'an, and learn the teachings of Islam. When explaining the Qur'an to the children, the sheik of the mosque had to translate from Arabic into Tashelhit for them, as most of the children were not yet able to understand or speak Arabic.

When Karim joined primary school in his village at the age of seven, he had already memorized parts of the Qur'an and the hadith (the sayings of Muhammad). Even so, he still attended the madrasa, and, under the tutelage of the sheik, the memorization of the Qur'an continued.

A NEW EXPERIENCE

The village's primary school had only three grades. After completing those three years, Karim's parents sent him to a different town, where he stayed with his grandfather in order to continue his primary and middle school education.

This constituted an important new phase in his life. Karim's interaction with his grandfather and some of his uncles, who were living in the same community, had a lasting impact on him. This family valued faith, intellect, politics, and hard work. Karim's grandfather was a sheik and faqih, one uncle was a judge, and another uncle was a notary. The house was home to a large library of quality books on various topics of Islam, literature, and history. Here, for the first time, Karim saw and read newspapers and magazines. And he listened in on discussions on topics such as Islamic intellectual policy and its role in society between his uncles and their friends.

During summer break, Karim still attended the madrasa in his home village. The memorizing of the Qur'an and the study of the hadith and the origins of Islam continued.

Karim's mother's greatest wish for him was that he become like her own father: A respected Islamic sheik and faqih. His father's ambitions, however, were more mundane. He hoped Karim would pursue and succeed in a secular trade.

THE SEARCH BEGINS IN CASABLANCA

For five years, Karim stayed with his grandfather. Then he moved to Casablanca, the large port city in central-western Morocco and the country's most important industrial center. His uncle ran a food shop in this city. Karim stayed with him and continued his middle and high school education.

It was here in 1966 that he made his first contact with the Christian faith. Karim was listening to the radio and was switching back and forth between different stations. In the process, he stumbled upon a radio station that was broadcasting a discussion on the topic of Christianity. Karim did not know that this was a Christian radio station. He thought it was an ordinary radio station hosting a discussion about religions in general.

The next day he listened in again. This time he realized that this was a Christian radio station.

At the end of the program, the broadcaster addressed the listeners.

"If you have any questions about Christianity, or if you would like to receive a calendar from us, please do not hesitate to write to us."

The address given by the broadcaster was located somewhere in France. Karim's interest had been roused. He wrote to them, and two weeks later he received their reply in the mail. They had sent him a small calendar with Bible verses as well as a coupon for a Bible study course.

WHAT IS THE TRUTH?

Karim considered Jews and Christians to be infidels, but he was interested in learning more about their beliefs. He had an inquisitive mind. So he subscribed to the Bible course and took part in it for several months.

In parallel, he became a regular visitor at the local library. He read famous Qur'anic and Muslim commentaries, such as the works of the well-known medieval Muslim philosophers, theologians, and scientists, including Ibn Rushd and the works of Al-Ghazali, the prominent reformer of the Muslim faith!

He also read up on some of the most prominent theological debates within Sunni Islam, such as between the Ash'aris—who believe one should attempt to give a rational and coherent account of Islam—and the Mu'tazila—who hold that reason is subordinate to revelation. He also read the Al-Milal wa al-Nihal, "the Book of Sects and Creeds," written by Muhammad al Shahrastani in 1128 and is widely viewed as the first systematic scholarly study of religion.

At the same time, he addressed his questions about—or, rather, his criticisms of—Christianity to Brother Youssef, the coordinator of the Bible study course.

"Why do you believe in four different gospels?"

"What about the falsification of the Bible?"

"Why do Christians believe in three gods?"

"How dare you say that God has a son?"

With a lot of patience and respect, Brother Youssef answered Karim's questions, concerns, and criticisms. His attitude of love and kindness had a great impact on Karim. It even led him to reflect about his own way of discussing and debating.

The discussions left Karim deeply confused on the inside about what he had heard and been taught from earliest childhood on.

What was right? What was wrong? What was the truth?

He prayed to God for guidance. "God, give me certainty, if Islam is the truth, or if Jesus Christ is the truth, give me peace about that!"

THE BIBLE STUDY GROUP

In the midst of this whirlwind of confusion, he received a letter from Brother Youssef. He asked him if he would be willing to meet a Christian believer in person, in order to speak about the questions and doubts that were weighing so heavily on him. Without hesitation, Karim agreed. It took a while, but eventually he received the address of a home in Casablanca.

Karim went to the address. It turned out to be the home of a missionary couple from the United States. Mr. Daoud spoke excellent Arabic and even with a Moroccan accent. Although he was ill that day, he invited Karim to come inside and engaged in a conversation with him.

"Every Tuesday, from seven to eight in the evening, we meet with a group of young people and study the Holy Bible. Would you like to join us?" Mr. Daoud asked.

"God, give me certainty, if Islam is the truth, or if Jesus Christ is the truth, give me peace about that!"

Two weeks later, Karim joined the group. There were seven other young people present. They read from the Bible, and then the group discussed what they had just read. An atmosphere of peace and harmony was tangible.

Karim started to regularly attend this study group, and he began to develop friendships with the other participants.

After about four months, Mr. Daoud approached Karim and two of the other young people in the study group. "I would like to invite the three of you to special study sessions. Please, from now on, come and meet with us on Friday evenings."

They accepted his invitation. In these Friday evening study sessions, they were introduced to two Bible teachers who would eventually become very dear to Karim: Brother Abdul-Karim and Brother Si Muhammad.

As he listened to them week after week, their expositions of the wonderful truths of the Word of God had a great influence on Karim. He even began to think of himself as a Christian, even though he still did not really understand what it meant to be a Christian.

But the fact of the matter was that Brother Youssef from France and Brother Abdul-Karim and Brother Si Muhammad in Casablanca had made an indelible impression on him. He wanted and wished to be like them.

BUT WHAT ABOUT YOU AND CHRIST?

During the summer of 1968, the topics dealt with in the study groups were the forgiveness of sin, the need for a personal decision for Christ, and assurance of salvation. One Friday evening after a study session, Brother Abdul-Karim and Karim went for a stroll together through the streets of Casablanca. Their conversation centered around what had been spoken about earlier in the Bible study group.

"How do you feel about the Christian faith?" Brother Abdul-Karim inquired. "Have you made a decision for Christ yet?"

This line of inquiry somewhat baffled Karim.

"I see myself as a Christian! I have studied the Bible for a long time. We have had many discussions on biblical topics. I know a lot about Christian doctrine and the Christian faith. That is why I say I'm a Christian!"

"That's all fine and good," Abdul-Karim replied. "You have knowledge and information about Christianity because you have studied the matter, as one could study any topic. But my question concerns your heart. Do you have faith in your heart, or is it just in your head? What about you and Christ? If you were to die today, would you be sure that you would go to heaven?"

"If you asked me this question with reference to Islam, as a Muslim, it would trouble me," Karim said, "because even if I made every effort possible—prayers, fasting, giving of alms, good deeds, performing the hajj—Paradise would still not be guaranteed to me. Only Allah knows.

"But the question of assurance of salvation seems to me to be different in Christianity. Didn't Christ himself say, 'Whoever believes in me, though he die, yet shall he live'? Didn't he tell the thief on the cross, 'Truly I tell you, today you will be with me in paradise'? It seems to me that Christ speaks about certainty, and not about a 'perhaps' or 'Allah knows'!"

Abdul-Karim was still not satisfied with Karim's answer.

"You see, you are right. All that knowledge is good. But it is still only theory. But the essence of being a Christian is not a mental matter! It is not about being with Christians. It is not a matter of a study of faith or an intellectual understanding. Being a Christian is really a matter of the heart, it is a personal life decision for Christ!"

They came to the corner of the street they were walking along, and each one of the two went their own way home.

FINDING CERTAINTY

That night, Karim sat down and pondered everything that had occupied him so much these last couple of months: Islam, Christianity, the Bible, all the studies, the arguments, and discussions.

In the end, it all boiled down to that question Abdul-Karim had asked him, "What about you and Christ?"

He bowed down and for the first time, from the bottom of his heart, he prayed and asked the Lord for the forgiveness of his sin and salvation. He prayed the prayer of the thief hanging on the cross: "Jesus, remember me when you come into your kingdom."

When he woke up the next morning, he sensed within himself a hitherto unknown peace and calm. All doubt and confusion had vanished from his mind and thoughts.

At the next Friday study session, Karim told what had happened to him. Everyone greatly rejoiced with him. He also wrote to Brother Youssef in France, thanking him for his crucial spiritual input.

Brother Karim joined a small local church and was baptized soon afterward.

HOW IT ALL CONTINUED

Family relations suddenly became very difficult for Brother Karim. Upon learning that he had become a Christian, his parents were very angry. Karim's sisters asked the local sheik whether it was halal (lawful, permissible) for **When he woke up the next morning, he sensed within himself a hitherto unknown peace and calm.** them to eat the food he prepared, or for their children to sit with Karim's children. One of his uncles revoked the engagement of his daughter to Karim's brother. He considered it haram (a taboo, forbidden) to deal with a family whose son had become an infidel.

Thankfully, Brother Karim was spared overtly violent reactions from family members, and, over time, most of the family relationships improved again.

In 1972, the police raided and closed the church that Brother Karim attended. Karim himself was called in for questioning. Being questioned by the police would later become an occurrence he grew accustomed to.

That same year he committed his life to full-time ministry, and in 1973, he enrolled in Bible college in Lebanon. He returned to Morocco in 1976, and since then, Karim and his wife have been pioneer missionaries there. During the last forty years, Karim has crisscrossed the country countless times from north to south and from east to west preaching the good news.

Also, just as he himself had first heard the gospel via airwaves, Brother Karim became a gospel radio broadcaster, bringing the gospel message through the radio in Arabic and his native Tashelhit language to his beloved fellow Moroccans. By the grace of God and as a fruit of his labors, there exists today a network of small underground house churches throughout Morocco.

HOW DOES ONE BECOME A MUSLIM?

It is very easy to become a Muslim. All it takes is an individual's confession of the shahada, the Islamic creed and the first of the five pillars of Islam: "There is no god but Allah; Muhammad is the messenger of Allah." Anyone who confesses this is considered a Muslim. Islam believes that all children born in the world are generically born as Muslims, even those children who are born to parents of other faiths, like Christians, since the whole world belongs to Allah. A Muslim man is allowed to marry a Christian or Jewish woman, but the children have to be raised as Muslims.

By contrast, the Bible teaches that no person is born a Christian. "God does not have grandchildren," as the popular saying goes. In fact, it takes a rebirth to become a Christian, that is, a child of God! Jesus taught this to Nicodemus in John 3. A person is born again and becomes a Christian when he or she makes a personal commitment of faith to Jesus Christ. Just like Brother Karim had to do.

CHAPTER 7

Thirty-Five Miles through the Bush in One Night

Brother Adamu
KENYA

RUN!

His sister warned him. It was his own grave that had been dug there, outside his home village in northern Kenya.

"If you do not escape tonight, you will certainly be killed!" she told him. "Run!"

The closest missionary lived thirty-five miles away. It would be a run through the dusty and thorny Savannah in the darkness of the night. There were lions and hyenas.

That night, Adamu escaped. He was twelve years old.

AFRICAN BEAUTY

The East African country of Kenya is host to some of the most stunning wildlife and nature scenes that the continent of Africa has to offer. It has numerous and large national parks to preserve this beauty and make it accessible to admirers of the Creator.

In Kenya's southwest corner, we find Lake Victoria, the world's second largest fresh water lake behind Lake Superior in North America. The region is also home to Africa's highest mountain peaks: Mount Kilimanjaro (5,895 meters/19,341 feet) is found right across Kenya's southern border in Tanzania. Africa's second highest peak, Mount Kenya, is found right in its center, and is located just ten miles south of the equator. When German missionaries Johannes Rebmann and Johann Krapf first laid sight on these mountains in the middle of the ninteenth century, they could not believe their eyes: snow-covered peaks in the middle of Africa! No wonder that their reports back home to Europe were at first not deemed credible.[1]

The country is bisected horizontally by the equator and vertically by the 38th meridian, which divides Kenya into two starkly distinct halves. The western portion is marked by a series of rising hills and mountain plateaus, while the eastern portion gently drops down to sea level at the coast, where Kenya borders the Indian Ocean. While parts of Kenya's East and South display some excellent farming opportunity with fertile soils and good annual precipitation, its North and Northeast are decidedly more arid. The vegetation of its red desert soil is sparse, and there is a constant danger of drought and famine. The availability of water is the limiting factor for habitation and survival in these regions.

ISLAMIC TERRORISM
AND LITERATURE EVANGELISTS

Kenya is a predominantly Christian country with about three-fourths of the population claiming allegiance to one of the various Christian denominations. Kenya's arid North and Northeast, however, display a very different picture. These are the home grounds to Kenya's sizeable Muslim minority. A very strict adherence to Islam is the hallmark of the people groups living here. The northeast border region to neighboring Somalia is also ground zero for the recruitment and training operations of the Somali-based Islamist terrorist group al-Shabaab. Al-Shabaab means "the youth for Allah." Al-Shabaab has been responsible for several high-profile terrorist attacks in Kenya during the last couple of years. In April of 2015, al-Shabaab-affiliated gunmen stormed the Garissa University College and took hostages from the student body. The hostages were interviewed: Muslim students were allowed to leave, while Christian students were retained and shot on the spot.

In recent years, it has become too dangerous for Westerners to travel to these Muslim regions of northern Kenya, much less to do missionary work there. Yet, today, there exists an army of volunteers—over one thousand of them, many of who are former Muslims—who, packed with evangelistic literature, are visiting village after village on foot and bringing the good news of salvation in Jesus Christ to Muslims in the north of Kenya.

A number of them have had to pay the ultimate price for their courageous actions and were killed by Muslim extremists who were angered by the spread of the gospel. Yet for every one who was murdered, even more have risen up and volunteered to take their place. The coordinator of this literature gospel outreach is Brother Adamu.

LEARNING THE QUR'AN

Brother Adamu knows these regions well. He was born in 1964 in a small village in Northern Kenya where his father held a position of honor in the village mosque. His birth was an answer to prayer for his strict Muslim parents: his father had pleaded with Allah to give him a son and, in return, he would meticulously guide this son in the ways of Allah.

There exists an army of volunteers who are visiting village after village on foot and bringing the good news of salvation in Jesus Christ to Muslims in the north of Kenya.

At the age of three, Adamu was sent to the madrasa (Qur'anic school), where he was expected to memorize the Muslim Holy Book in Arabic. So, every day at 5:30 a.m., his mother accompanied him to the madrasa. Since he didn't know Arabic, he did not understand a word of what he had to learn. But according to Islamic theology, the Qur'an should only be recited in Arabic, its original language.

When Adamu attended primary school, he still got up at 5:30 every morning to go to the madrasa, then rushed home at 7:30 in order to quickly eat breakfast and be ready to attend school at 8:00 a.m. During the afternoons, he resumed his Qur'anic studies. Adamu had been meticulously trained to know his obligations and he strictly adhered to them.

During his time in secondary school, Adamu devoted each

morning and each evening to memorizing the Islamic Scriptures.

THE BIBLE AS TOILET PAPER

When Adamu was twelve years old, a European-looking man made his appearance in the village square and disrupted the village's daily activities. It was Brother Anderson, an American missionary who at the age of seventy was still traveling throughout Kenya in order to spread the gospel and even ventured into the country's North.

Brother Anderson had brought some books and schooling materials with him, which he donated to the village school. The headmaster of the school was glad to receive him. The missionary had also brought something else. He had traveled with a stack of Bibles and donated one Bible to every child in the school.

Adamu knew that as a Muslim he was not supposed to possess a Bible. Yet, it would have been culturally unacceptable to publicly show disrespect toward an elderly person by refusing to accept a gift offered to him. The cultural taboo of disrespecting the elderly superseded the religious taboo of accepting a Bible. So, Adamu and the other children took the Bible from Brother Anderson.

But Adamu already had an idea of what he could do with the Bible he received. The family had an outhouse at their home, so Adamu decided it would be best used as toilet paper. That resolved the matter. The Bible represented an important element of the Christian faith, and Adamu as a devout Muslim was glad he, in a small way, was able to harm Christianity through the destruction of this Bible.

Adamu apparently was not the only well-trained Muslim child in the village. The sight of partially destroyed Bibles became a common thing in the village over the next couple of weeks.

JOHN 3 AND A CAN OF CORNED BEEF

Three months later, the missionary returned to the village and was invited to the school again.

"Where are your Bibles?" he asked all the children who were gathered in the school assembly.

Brother Anderson's question was met with silence. He was able to imagine what had happened to the Bibles, so he made his second attempt more witty.

"I have brought some Bibles for you again," he said. "This time, together with the Bible, you will also receive a pen and coloring pencils."

"However, there is one condition for you to receive the pen and the coloring pencils," the missionary continued. "Only those who learn chapter three of the Gospel of John by heart will receive them. And something else: The first ten students to do so will also receive a can of corned beef!"

The race was on. This was an offer the village children couldn't resist. They had never possessed coloring pencils of their own! Adamu took the Bible, hurried home, and started memorizing John 3. He was determined to be among the first ten students to do so and win that can of corned beef to give to his mother. It would be the first time in his life that he would be able to give a gift to her. It was handy that he had been trained so well in the madrasa to learn long passages of text by heart.

Three days later, Adamu went to the missionary. Indeed, he succeeded to recite John 3 without making any mistakes. He received his well-deserved pen, the coloring pencils, and the can of corned beef. Proudly, he ran home and surprised his mother with the treat. The second Bible he had received from Brother Anderson went to its now already-familiar destination in the outhouse.

MOCKERY TURNS TO COMPASSION

But something had changed. Adamu had put sweat and effort into learning a whole chapter of the Bible by heart. His personal investment prickled his curiosity about this book of the Christians. From time to time, he would pick it up and read some of it, starting with the Gospels in the New Testament.

At first, nothing he read about Jesus in the gospels really gripped him. As he continued to read and came to the account of the crucifixion, he cheered on what happened to Christ. Later, he told the story to his school buddies. Together, they laughed heartily about the murder of Jesus. In his imagination, Adamu saw himself in the story, gathering with the crowd and helping the soldiers drive the nails through Jesus' hands and feet.

Yet, as time progressed, he realized that, somehow, he was not able to shake off the memories and impressions of his Bible reading. Slowly but surely, the biblical text made its unfailing impact on his heart and mind. Particularly the cry of Jesus on the cross, "My God, my God, why have you forsaken me?" had etched itself into his consciousness. Slowly, his mockery and hatred of Jesus turned into compassion and pity. He wanted Jesus' cruel ordeal to stop.

Adamu's heart had been touched. He experienced a new and unknown inward strength. He wanted to know and read more about Jesus. The negativity toward the Bible and Christianity, with which he had been indoctrinated by his Muslim elders from his earliest memories, was gone.

Slowly, his mockery and hatred of Jesus turned into compassion and pity.

Why did Jesus have to die on the cross? He had so many questions.

"WILL I HAVE TO GO TO HELL IF I BELIEVE IN JESUS?"

When the missionary returned for a third time a few months later, Adamu seized the chance to speak to him about the questions that absorbed him. Brother Anderson addressed the issues in depth. As best as possible, he explained to the young boy the biblical truths: Jesus, the Son of God, died for us. God laid the punishment for our sins on Him so that we can be forgiven. His death was not the end—on the third day, He rose from the dead! And guess what? Those who believe in Christ and entrust their lives to Him will not be sentenced to hell but enjoy a glorious eternity with God in heaven.

The possibility of escaping the judgement of Allah and not be exposed to the flames of hell caught Adamu's attention. As a well-informed Muslim, he knew that the Qur'an teaches that everyone, even the most devout Muslim and those who Allah eventually will allow to go to paradise, will likely have to go through the flames of hell first (Sura 19:71).

The thought that he should one day be exposed to the fires of hell frightened Adamu. As a young child, he had a type of skin disease. There were no regular doctors in their village or even a hospital within reach. Thus, the traditional African village shaman was tasked with the treatment of the disease. This "treatment" consisted of burning the affected spots on Adamu's skin with fire!

This utterly painful and traumatizing experience had left Adamu terrified of fire. And he was horrified that as a Muslim, there probably was no way for him to escape going through the fires of hell after he died. And now this missionary spoke of a possibility to escape the fires of hell!

"Is it really a sure thing that I will not go to hell if I believe in and follow Jesus?" he asked the missionary.

"It is sure as sure can be," replied Brother Anderson. He recited John 3:16: "For God so loved the world that he gave his one and only Son [Jesus, who died on the cross for our sins] so that whoever believes in him shall not perish but have eternal life.

"You do not have to go through hell to reach heaven! Jesus paid the price!"

Twelve-year-old Adamu prayed together with Brother Anderson and personally trusted Jesus for the forgiveness of his sins and his salvation. What inner peace and joy he now experienced; he was now free from fear!

PERSECUTION

Outwardly, however, this was the start of many troubles for Adamu. Jesus said, "In this world you will have trouble. But take heart! I have overcome the world" (John 16:33).

How would he tell his father that he did not want to attend the madrasa anymore or learn the Qur'an by heart? Adamu was scared of his reaction. Nevertheless, he went and told him that he had become a Christian and would not be attending Islamic school anymore.

His father's reaction was furious and sparked the start of many violent beatings. He would put his foot on Adamu's neck to hold him down as he beat him. Even the teacher of the madrasa joined in with the punishment.

Twelve-year-old Adamu prayed together with Brother Anderson and personally trusted Jesus. What inner peace and joy he now experienced; he was now free from fear!

His father would also frequently beat and mistreat his mother. He accused her of not having raised his son right. These dramatic and traumatic experiences etched themselves into his soul.

There exists an unwritten rule in the African culture of Adamu's village. If a father is seen violently hitting his child, a passerby has the right to intervene and de-escalate the situation. Yet in one instance, more than forty people stood and watched how Adamu's father beat him, but not one single person intervened. Adamu had never felt more helpless than in that moment.

AN ESCAPE AND A NEW BEGINNING

One day, his father called for a meeting with the village elders. "Adamu is not my son anymore. He has left Islam. I have to remove the shame from my family's name. He is not allowed to bear my name anymore, nor can he live."

He showed the elders a grave he had already dug for his son. A ceremonial bull was slaughtered and a fire was lit. All the elders threw something into the fire, thereby expressing their agreement to the death sentence that had been pronounced for Adamu.

Adamu's older sister witnessed the ceremony and warned him. "Run, you must run!"

Adamu knew about a missionary who lived approximately thirty-five miles away from his village. In the darkness of that very night, he fled and traveled the thirty-five miles on foot, right through the dangerous African bush. Early the next morning, he reached the missionary.

The missionary helped him find Brother Anderson, who was living in Nairobi, the capital of Kenya. Upon hearing what had happened to him, Brother Anderson and his wife agreed to take him in and they raised him as a son. He stayed with them for nine years, until the elderly couple tragically died in a car accident.

But now Adamu was already a young adult and able to look after himself. He married a beautiful young lady—also a convert from Islam—and enlisted in the Kenyan army. There he rose through the ranks and became a training supervisor in the artillery.

THE GOSPEL CANNOT BE STOPPED

While still alive, Brother Anderson had always told him, "Do not forget northern Kenya! Do not forget your home village!"

The thought of his unreached relatives who were still living in the darkness of Islam haunted Adamu. And it was more than just his relatives who needed to hear the gospel. The whole Islamic part of northern Kenya and beyond needed to hear the good news of deliverance and salvation in Jesus Christ.

Adamu quit the army and joined a Bible college. Later, he became a coworker with our mission organization, Call of Hope, and assisted in their literature evangelism program to Muslims all over Kenya and eastern Africa. In 2002, he became the head of the Kenyan branch of Call of Hope. From its main office in Nairobi, Brother Adamu is now overseeing a project that reaches tens of thousands of spiritually hungry Muslims every year with the good news of salvation in Jesus Christ. That same good news from the Bible that saved him from the fear of hell.

They are willing to take the risk; for they, just like Brother Adamu, have found eternal life through faith in Jesus.

Adamu has also journeyed back to his home village. During a time of extreme drought and famine for northern Kenya, he was able to deliver a substantial amount of aid to his home village with the help of Call of Hope. Today, Brother Adamu is a respected person in his village, and several of his relatives have also accepted Christ as Savior. Adamu's own brother was even martyred for his faith in Jesus.

The thousand-plus volunteers who are participating in the

literature outreach program to Islamic northern Kenya, which Brother Adamu is overseeing, know that their lives are always in danger by Muslim extremists who do not want the gospel message to reach their regions and villages. Yet, they are willing to take the risk; for they, just like Brother Adamu, have found eternal life through faith in Jesus. And this is a message so wonderful that they cannot remain silent.

DOES ISLAM PROVIDE ASSURANCE OF SALVATION?

Islam is a works-based religion. The committed Muslim hopes that through the accumulation of good works, they can gain the favor of Allah and that their good deeds in the day of judgment will outweigh their bad deeds. Good deeds are those which belong to the so-called five pillars of Islam. These pillars include: saying the shahada, the Muslim confession of faith; reciting the Islamic prayer five times a day; giving alms to the poor of the Muslim community; fasting for thirty days during the month of Ramadan; and performing the hajj, the pilgrimage to Mecca, at least once.

Being a good Muslim according to Islamic theology is no guarantee that a person will escape hell and be granted entry into paradise. In fact, no Muslim can be sure of their personal eternal salvation, and to foster such an assurance would be sin. It is left up to Allah's discretion whom he allows entry into paradise. Even the prophet Muhammad himself was afraid of death.[2] The devout Muslim's desired inner state regarding the assurance of salvation is to find the perfect balance between hope and fear.

Most devout Muslims that one encounters have one big desire: "I want to go to paradise." They try to follow all the Muslim rules and regulations, but they will never know for sure if they will go to paradise or not. Even many Muslim scholars become desperate, because they do not know where they will go after death. How wonderful it is that we are able to talk to Muslims about the assurance of salvation that we have and that they can have, too, through Jesus!

CHAPTER 8

The Lion of Christ

Brother Asad
INDIA

THE PILGRIMAGE TO AJMER

His parents had named him Asad Allah: The Lion of Allah.

The teenage boy had embarked on a twenty-four hour train ride with his grandfather, the great maulana (Muslim scholar), and four of his grandfather's disciples.

They were on a pilgrimage to Ajmer, Rajasthan, in order to visit the tomb of the Muslim saint and famous teacher of Sunni Sufism,[1] Khwājah Muʿīn al-Dīn Chishtī. Hundreds of thousands of Muslim pilgrims flock to this holy Muslim site for prayer and worship every year.

They stayed in Ajmer for three days, and most of that time was spent worshiping in the grand hall of the sanctuary.

Asad couldn't help but notice that many of the pilgrims they met showed great reverence toward his grandfather. In bringing him along, Asad's grandfather wanted to communicate to him: Follow in my footsteps, and you too, can become a famous maulana. You can have a great following and many disciples will flock to your teachings. People will even kiss your feet; they will bring you offerings; they will treat you with the utmost respect. All this honor and wealth can be yours!

It was an overwhelming experience for Asad. As they made their way back home, he knew more than ever that his name was his destiny: to lead the Muslim faithful and bring glory to Allah.

And yet, he was not able to completely shake off his lurking doubts.

INCREDIBLE INDIA

The Indian subcontinent fills the greater part of South Asia. With almost 1.4 billion citizens, India will likely soon overtake China to become the world's most populous country. Roughly every sixth person in the world is living there. India is also the world's largest democracy. Hindi and English are the country's official languages, but the different provinces boast of a great variety of other spoken languages. The Republic of India is made up of twenty-nine states and six union territories.

The average person from the West who visits India usually falls within one of two categories: love it or hate it.

Some love it: The total otherness of India compared to the US, Canada, or Europe; its rich cultural heritage and history; its fascinating cities, cultural sites, and temples; the friendliness and hospitality of the Indian people; the peculiarities of a rich Indian cuisine.

Others hate it: The overpopulated Indian megacities teeming with masses of people; the poor traffic conditions and hopelessly congested streets; the need to constantly protect oneself against infectious diseases; the abject poverty of large parts of the population visibly on display everywhere. No one enjoys the sight of slumlike housing from the window of one's luxury hotel room.

WHY ARE THERE SO MANY MUSLIMS IN INDIA?

When thinking of India in religious terms, "Hinduism" is the term that pops into most people's minds, and justifiably so. It is the motherland of the Hindu religion. Yet, India is also home to about two hundred million Muslims. Incredibly, in terms of sheer numbers, this makes India the country with the third largest Muslim population in the world. Number one is Indonesia, number two Pakistan, and number three—India.

Because India is a majority Hindu nation, the importance of evangelizing to India's Muslims is sometimes overlooked by mission organizations. Another reason for this could be that mission work among Muslims is often more difficult and more dangerous than evangelizing to followers of other religions.

But why are there so many Muslims in India? History provides us with the answer to this question. For centuries, Muslim dynasties ruled different parts of India. The Muslim conquest of and settlement in India began in the eighth century. Many of the Muslim dynasties also pursued a policy of forced Islamization of the indigenous Hindu population. An estimated eighty million Hindus were massacred by their Muslim overlords over the centuries.[2]

European colonization slowly but surely brought an end to Muslim rule in India. In 1876, Queen Victoria of England was officially declared the Empress of India. British rule lasted up to the middle of the twentieth century. During this time, India, Pakistan, and Bangladesh all formed one country. When Indian independence was finally realized in 1947, a partition took place, which happened largely along religious lines: India became the majority Hindu state—while still hosting considerable religious minorities of Muslims, Christians, and others—and Pakistan and Bangladesh were essentially Muslim.

Still today, one encounters the presence of Islam everywhere in India. There are large mosques, famous pilgrimage sites, and well-respected Islamic scholars.

A FAMILY OF RELIGION AND RICHES

Brother Asad was born into a wealthy and devout Muslim family in the northeastern Indian province of West Bengal in 1962.

Asad's grandfather was a famous Indian maulana (Muslim religious scholar), who attracted thousands of Muslims to hear his teachings each year. People from all over India came to his grandfather for prayer and to become his disciple. When these people visited him, they brought along gifts: gifts of gold, silver, animals, and other valuables. These gifts made the family exceedingly rich. It seems like the "Christian" phenomenon of a wealthy televangelist is nothing new!

Every year in March, Asad's grandfather conducted a large spiritual seminar. At least ten thousand of his faithful disciples would attend. The attendees of this seminar would also bring along their gifts. Even some people of Hindu faith would come and listen to his grandfather's teachings. Some subsequently converted to Islam and became his disciples.

Unsurprisingly, they were the richest family in the area.

As his grandfather grew older, he had to think of a suitable successor for his position as a well-respected maulana. Asad's mother had seven brothers, and his father had three brothers. But none of them were particularly interested in religion and would not consider following in the maulana's footsteps. For this reason, his grandfather chose Asad. He decided to train him up as his future successor.

The young Asad was sent to the madrasa at the prestigious Aliah University in Kolkata, where his grandafather formerly taught, to receive a solid religious education.

With great passion, Asad threw himself into his studies. The thought of following in his admired grandfather's footsteps motivated him. In ten years at the madrasa, Asad studied twelve different subjects in-depth that relate to the practice and teaching of Islam, including Arabic grammar, Arabic literature, history of Islam, and the Qur'an itself. His discipline and careful attention made him excel in all the classes that he took.

In his free time, Asad often accompanied his grandfather to visits and meetings. People who met him were astonished to see the boy's eagerness in learning about Islam and the practice of making disciples.

QUESTIONS THAT CONCERN JESUS

During his studies of the Qur'an at Aliah, Asad also came to know about Jesus for the first time. He read some astonishing things about Him in the Qur'an. There, Jesus and His mother Mary were characterized as holy people. Moreover, Jesus possessed special powers and was able to perform miracles.

No miracles are recorded of the prophet Muhammad in the Qur'an, and the Qur'an tells that Muhammad had to ask Allah for forgiveness for his sins.[3] Yet there was no record of Jesus having to seek forgivness in the Qu'ran. This was confusing to Asad. Doubts started to creep into his mind.

> The Qur'an tells that Muhammad had to ask Allah for forgiveness for his sins. Yet there was no record of Jesus having to seek forgivness in the Qu'ran.

He asked his grandfather concerning the questions he had with regard to Jesus and Muhammad.

Instead of giving him an explanation, his grandfather replied, "Never allow yourself to think negatively of either Muhammad or the Qur'an. Muhammad was the last prophet sent by Allah. Never doubt the Qur'an."

This answer did not resolve his confusion. During his time at the madrasa, Asad's questions regarding Jesus and Muhammad continued to build. The discussions with and answers from his teachers did not bring any clarity.

Sometimes, the whole issue overwhelmed him. It felt as if his brain became paralyzed.

One day, Asad secretly left the madrasa and went to the town Furfura Sharif, north of Kolkata. This was a Muslim holy place and a destination for Muslim pilgrims. Asad knew that the imams there were considered especially well-educated. He wanted to speak to them about these matters that tormented him on the inside.

When he arrived there, he addressed his questions to the head imam.

Instead of providing him with an answer, the imam became angry and started to curse him. This was not what Asad had hoped for.

The madrasa had reported to his family that Asad had gone missing. After two days of searching, Asad's family found him in Furfura Sharif and brought him back home.

Back home, everyone tried to assuage his doubts. "Jesus is not a god. Don't think about the matter again!"

Once, Asad's grandfather took him along on a special pilgrimage trip to Ajmer. For three days, they participated in grand religious activities. Asad was stunned to see the position of honor and prestige that his grandfather held among the pilgrims.

The message was clear: All that could one day be his, if he so chose.

Asad returned to the madrasa and continued his studies. His doubts had not been cleared, but for the moment, he suppressed them.

LURES OF THE SECULAR LIFE

At seventeen years old, Asad had completed his ten-year curriculum at the madrasa. Next, he joined a secular school in order to obtain his regular high school degree. After that, he enrolled in the Midnapore College in Kolkata, from which he graduated after two years of studies in 1981.

Because Asad had been chosen to became a famous maulana in the future, he was prohibited from participating in many common activities: No sports allowed, no entertainment, no watching of movies, no talking to girls. Soccer had always particularly interested him, and while he was still at the madrasa, he sometimes played secretly. That gave him great satisfaction.

Upon entering college, he suddenly had the freedom to do all the things previously forbidden to him: He could play soccer, watch movies, and talk with girls.

He kept all this a secret from his family.

At college, Asad also had his first taste of success. He fought and won in the elections of the Student Federation of India, and he became the vice president of the college student government.

The power he now wielded and the respect he earned through this position made him hungry for more. He dreamt of becoming both rich and powerful, and quickly.

He asked to postpone taking his grandfather's position in order to have additional time to pursue his own goals first.

To Asad, the best way to earn money and gain power in a short period of time seemed to be a career with the Indian police, followed by a switch into politics.

After graduating from college, Asad completed the six-month police training and was given a post as police inspector for traffic control. He was put in charge of a road checkpoint between the Indian provinces of West Bengal and Jharkhand.

Very quickly, his personal wealth increased. The trick was the bribes. When on duty, Asad would make as much or more money from bribes in one day than his monthly salary. Buses and trucks would pay him a bribe, so that he would allow them to pass the checkpoint without inspection.

A BIBLE INSTEAD OF A BRIBE

For three years, Asad remained at this checkpoint. Everything was going as planned. He had become a rich young man and had established connections to local politicians.

After three years, he was assigned to a different traffic checkpoint. The same routine continued there.

One day while on duty, Asad was checking a bus. He checked the whole bus and the bus driver's papers. Then he demanded a bribe from the driver.

"I am not a rich person, and I don't have any money on me. The only thing I can give you is a Bible. It is the most precious gift in the world. Please read it!" the bus driver replied.

Reluctantly, he took the Bible. Asad did not know it at the time, but the bus belonged to the ministry organization OM (Operation Mobilization).

A couple of months later, Asad and the bus driver—his name was Ramesh—met again at the checkpoint.

"Have you read the Bible yet?" Ramesh asked.

"I am a Muslim, and I will not read the Bible," Asad responded.

Ramesh was not satisfied with his answer.

"Jesus came for the people from all religions. Jesus is not a religion. He came to give us a new life! Please start reading the New Testament."

A couple of days later on a rainy day, Asad took off from work. He remembered the bus driver's suggestion, so he pulled out the Bible and read a couple of pages. However, he didn't really catch on to what he read and put the Bible away again.

FINDING NEW LIFE

Some time passed. Again, Asad and Brother Ramesh met at the same checkpoint.

"Jesus came for the people from all religions. Jesus is not a religion. He came to give us a new life!"

"Have you read the Bible yet?"

"I have, but it was not interesting to me, and I will not read it again."

"Please read the Gospel of John, and read it with a gentle and enquiring mind."

A few days later, as he had nothing else to do, Asad took the Bible and started reading the Gospel of John. This time around, what he read really gripped him. Within one week, he had read through the entire book. His interest increased. He read through all four Gospels. Then he read through the entire New Testament.

When Asad started reading through the New Testament for the second time, he also started attending the Sunday services of a local church. A real hunger for the Word of God had sprung up in his heart, so he also started reading the Old Testament. One Sunday, after the church service, he remained behind in the church yard and read through the entire book of Psalms.

More and more he began to understand what the Christian faith was all about. Finally, he was finding answers to the questions concerning this Jesus that he had harbored since his childhood!

On Christmas Eve of 1988, Asad attended an all-night prayer service at the church. On this occasion, he once again read the words from Scripture that are written in John 14:6:

> "Jesus answered, 'I am the way and the truth and the life. No one comes to the Father except through me.'"

That night, Asad accepted Jesus as his personal Savior and became a new person in Christ.

CONSEQUENCES

His conversion immediately had consequences to his everyday life. For example, he stopped taking bribes when on duty as a traffic police officer.

Asad's colleagues were underwhelmed by the change in his life. They resented it. Even his superiors didn't like it. They too had profited from his bribing schemes.

Every morning Asad now got up and prayed that God would help him lead a truthful life that day, and at the same time help him in the struggle with his colleagues.

After ten months of struggle and pressure, Asad resigned from his job with the police. Instead, he intended to join a Bible college.

He went back home to his family and told them about his conversion. They thought that he had gone mad. In fact, they took him to see a psychiatrist!

The fact that he had become a Christian was particularly shocking to his parents and his grandfather. They had invested so much in him—Asad Allah, the Lion of Allah—in order to train him up as a future maulana.

News of his conversion to Christianity quickly spread; some of his grandfather's disciples came to convince Asad to return to the Muslim faith. When all their efforts proved vain, they turned to threats.

"If you don't give up Christianity and return to Islam, we will come and kill you."

Asad's grandfather knew that this was no empty threat. His life really was in grave danger. Therefore, he presented Asad with two choices: Either convert back to Islam and stay with the family, or else leave the family home forever.

A NEW BEGINNING

Asad chose to remain faithful to Christ and decided to leave. He met with his mother for one last time before his departure. For the next several decades, he was completely cut off from contact with his family and relatives. He left with nothing more than the clothes he wore. Since all the money he had previously earned had been placed into the family fund, it remained behind, and he was left with nothing.

He went first to nearby Kolkata and spent the night at the railway station. In the morning, not knowing where else to go, he boarded a train. Somehow the conductor never came to check on the tickets.

After three hours the train came to its final stop in a town in the very north of West Bengal. Asad disembarked and asked some local people if they knew of a church nearby. Indeed, there was one, about an hour's walk away.

The pastor of the church received him with friendship and listened to his story. He invited Asad to stay with him for a couple of months until the Bible college would take in new students.

His life really was in grave danger. Yet Asad chose to remain faithful to Christ and decided to leave.

He also arranged a job for him at the nearby hospital. The pay was eight Indian rupees per day. Previously, as a police officer, he had sometimes made as much as two thousand rupees per day. To live off his new income, Asad would skip breakfast and use six rupees to pay for lunch and dinner. In this way, he could save up two rupees per day for Bible college.

In April 1990, he received his baptism. Baptisms of Muslim converts were very rare in those days. The pastor who had agreed to baptize Asad feared the consequences from the Muslim community. When the time of the actual baptism came, the pastor was shaking with fear.

Seeing this, Asad entered the water first and invited the pastor to join him! "There is nothing to be afraid of," he said.

From now on, he introduced himself by a new name: Asad Masih, the Lion of Christ, the Messiah.

THE CALL TO MINISTRY

Brother Asad planned to join the ministry of OM India, since it had been through one of their staff that he had come to know Christ.

However, the pastor who baptized him objected. "I have been

praying since last year for someone to start an outreach ministry specifically among Muslims in India. I believe you are the answer to my prayers!"

Brother Asad took this as a personal call from God.

Next, he submitted his application to enter a Bible college in Kolkata. He passed the written admission test and was called in for a personal interview in front of the college staff.

"How do you intend to pay the college fees?" the Bible college director asked him.

Brother Asad had no money and no sponsor. "Jesus will take care of my fees," he said.

The entire faculty laughed heartily at his answer.

The principal responded, "You may start college next week, and we will take your fees from Jesus!"

As it later turned out, the Lord laid it on the heart of an anonymous donor from the United States to pay for Asad's first-year college fees. From his second year on, he was awarded a Bible college scholarship because of his good grades.

TRULY RICH

Early in 1992, Asad married Shuvra, a young lady from Brahman Hindu background who he himself had led to Christ. They were as poor as church mice and were not even able to afford proper rings or a wedding dress. Together, they started a ministry among Muslims in India. It was a humble start. In October 1995, they were able to hold their first baptism camp, and Brother Asad baptized twenty-seven former Muslims.

Today, he runs a ministry across several Indian states. Through his ministry, hundreds of house churches have formed and more than seventeen thousand former Muslims have confessed their faith in Christ through baptism. The work is still continuing.

Asad may have forsaken the honor of men and millions of rupees in earthly riches, but he is, in fact, a truly rich man in the eyes of God.

After three decades of silence, God brought about reconciliation for Asad and his family. In 2019, Brother Asad was able to reconnect with one of his brothers. Later that same year, that brother and his family received Christ! This opened the door to reestablish contact with other relatives and family members. He began a Bible study group for family members, in which his own mother joined. In early 2020, Brother Asad held a two-day Bible seminar with thirty-nine of his relatives. Of those who attended, ten decided to follow Christ and asked to be baptized.

Asad may have forsaken the honor of men and millions of rupees in earthly riches, but he is, in fact, a truly rich man in the eyes of God.

CAN I USE THE QUR'AN TO REACH MUSLIMS FOR CHRIST?

Brother Asad first heard about Jesus by reading the Qur'an, which contains multiple references to Jesus (Isa) and other biblical figures such as Adam, Noah, Abraham, Job, Jonah, John the Baptist, and Mary. Muhammad placed himself in a long line of successive prophets, which Allah supposedly had sent to different peoples throughout history.[4] It was Muhammad's claim that he was the last and final of all prophets,[5] and that through his ministry, Allah was confirming the ministry of the previous prophets, as reported by the writings of the "people of the book," i.e. the Jews and Christians.[6]

What the Qur'an reports about the stories of biblical figures bears some similarities to what we read about them in the Bible, but it also differs wildly in many details.

Jesus (Isa) is viewed as one of the many prophets of Allah. The Qur'an speaks about his virgin birth and that Allah created Isa in the womb of Mary.[7] It also reports that "with the permission of Allah" Jesus performed many miracles.[8] The Qur'an vehemently attacks and denies that Jesus is the Son of God and, as such, is God.[9] To assert that Allah would have a son would be the chief of all sins.[10] No, Jesus was merely a human and a prophet. Also, the Qur'an explicitly denies that Jesus died on the cross.[11]

Given that the Qur'an contains multiple allusions to biblical content, wouldn't it be a wise to use it to evangelize to Muslims?

Our response to this is: The references to biblical figures in the Qur'an have been the starting point for some Muslims on their journey to Christ. However, the Isa (Jesus) of the Qur'an is not Jesus of the Bible. And the Qur'an itself will never lead someone to faith in Christ, the Son of God. It provides no basis for such faith whatsoever. It explicitly denies the divinity of Christ and the Trinity. Allah of the Qur'an is not the same as the God of the Bible. Faith in Christ must always be founded on biblical truth and the exposition of Scripture.

CHAPTER 9

A Mullah Risks His Life for Christ

Brother Salman
INDIA and KASHMIR

THE SHARIA COURT CITATION

Several times already, Salman had refused to obey the order by the sharia court in Srinagar, the capital of Kashmir, to appear in trial. This time he knew that a continued refusal would result in severe consequences—the Muslim extremists threatened to abduct his two young girls.

What had happened? Someone had secretly filmed Brother Salman's baptism service, where he baptized former Muslims who now professed belief in Christ. Afterward, that video was posted on the internet, and Muslim leaders were notified. The sharia court convened and demanded Salman's appearance. According to Muslim sharia law, an apostate from Islam and those promoting apostasy receive capital punishment.

As he approached the court that day, Brother Salman did not know what would happen to him and his family.

KASHMIR—A REGION IN THE SQUEEZE BETWEEN INDIA AND PAKISTAN

Formerly one of India's largest states, the state of Jammu and Kashmir was downgraded to union territory by the central Indian government in 2019. Earlier that year, Islamist and separatist terrorists had conducted a massive suicide bombing, targeting Indian police forces. In its wake, the Indian and Pakistani militaries had clashed.

This action by the Indian government was just the latest in a long succession of attempts to try and bring stability and full Indian control to a province that has been marked by unrest and instability since the partition of India and Pakistan in 1947 (see the previous chapter). That partition did not clearly resolve the issue of Kashmiri allegiance, which up until then had been an independent entity under British rule. In the end, Kashmir was split between Pakistan and India along an armistice line.

Kashmir is India's only majority-Muslim region. Historically, by contrast, Kashmir was a tough land to capture for the Muslim invaders, who came to India from the eighth century onward. Only in the fourteenth century did it fall to Muslim control.

Today, the majority of the Kashmir's Muslim population

would prefer to live under Pakistani rather than Indian control. Their grievances against the central Indian government are often projected onto the local non-Muslim inhabitants, including Christians. This makes Christian missionary activity, already difficult in India as a whole, particularly challenging in Kashmir.

But this strife did not hold Brother Salman and his wife back from moving there in 1995 to spread the Word of God. The love of God compelled them to venture into this troubled region and risk their lives for the cause of the gospel. The remarkable thing is that formerly Brother Salman himself had been a persecutor of Christians!

RAISED TO BE A MULLAH

Salman grew up in a devoted Muslim family not far from the city of Lucknow in northern India. His parents took their Muslim faith very seriously. They did not even want their kids to associate with or play with the children of non-Muslim parents. Salman was not allowed to shake hands with those who did not believe in Muhammad and Allah. Coming into contact with anything non-Muslim was deemed unclean.

Muslims in northern India generally speak Urdu as their mother tongue. So, if Salman accidentally picked up a writing in another Indian language—in Hindi, for example, which is one of the main languages spoken by the Hindu population of northern India—he would throw it down again as quickly as possible. Reading something in a language that had no connection to Islam would render him ceremonially unclean, so he had been taught.

The family had ten children, and Salman was the second youngest of seven sons. His older sisters were not allowed to leave the home unaccompanied. Three of his older brothers became mullahs (Muslim religious leaders), and it was his parents' wish that Salman should follow that same path. Therefore, from the age of three on, he had to get up at 4:00 a.m. in order to get to the madrasa on time.

The learning schedule devoted itself to the same subject each day: learning the Qur'an by heart. This part of his childhood was very difficult for Salman. It is difficult for a boy of such young age to sit still and concentrate for hours and recite long passages.

Whenever he made mistakes in his recitations, his teacher beat him. Once he complained to his parents about the strictness of his madrasa teacher. Instead of sympathizing with him, he got an additional beating from his parents for complaining!

At the age of eight, Salman had memorized the Qur'an in its entirety.

THE ATTACK ON THE CHRISTIAN EVANGELISTS

Salman's parents raised him to love Islam and to hate followers of other religions. The most important thing was to read the Qur'an, to listen to and follow the advice of his Islamic teachers, and to become a defender of Islam!

As a youth, Salman already possessed all the outward marks of a young mullah: He had grown a beard and was dressed in the long, traditional gown that is worn by Islamic students. He wore a cap on his head and carried the misbaha (Islamic prayer beads) in his hand.

Salman received no secular education at all. After completing the madrasa curriculum when he was eight years old, he studied at various Islamic colleges for seven additional years. He was even sent to an Islamic institution in Iran in order to bring his religious education to perfection. Having completed all his religious studies when he was only twenty years old, he was appointed mullah of the central mosque in his hometown. There, he taught the Muslim faithful the teachings of the Qur'an and led them five times a day in the prescribed Islamic ritualistic prayer.

He hated everything Christian. He was known beyond the confines of his hometown for his hatred for Christians.

One day, a Christian outreach team distributed evangelistic literature right in front of the mosque where Salman was mullah.

Some of the Muslims who were entering the mosque brought the literature with them. When Salman saw what type of literature they had received, he was irate. How dare the evil Christians spread their corrupt propaganda right there at the mosque?

He mustered some of the young men who were present at the mosque. Together, they went outside and beat up this group of Christians who were distributing the literature. They also set fire to their van, which contained the literature stock.

After having completed their raid, Salman and his men returned to the mosque.

TOUCHED BY THE LOVE OF GOD
AND PERSECUTED HIMSELF

A couple of hours later, some of the Christians they had beat up earlier reappeared at the mosque. They wanted to see Salman. As he went to meet them, Salman was sure that they would be shaking with fear. To his astonishment, they appeared to be calm and collected.

"Sir, we just want to let you know that God loves you, that we also love you, and that we are praying for you. We would also like to give you this card."

The card they gave him had John 3:16 printed on it. "For God so loved the world, that he gave his only Son, that whoever believes in him shall not perish but have eternal life." Then they handed him a New Testament in Urdu.

Salman was stunned. He had expected nothing of the sort. This gesture by the Christian believers deeply touched him, and he was heartbroken that he had mistreated and persecuted people who loved and even prayed for their enemies!

The words from John 3:16 made a deep impression on him. Who was this Christian Jesus who claimed that He could secure him entry into paradise?

This experience became a turning point in Salman's life. He started to read the New Testament, which the group of Christians had given to him. What he read he compared to the teachings of Islam. The message of the love of God for all of humanity on display in Scripture gripped him. This was not characteristic of Allah in Islam. He had many questions for which he desired to find answers and continued to read the New Testament every day.

Salman's fellow mullahs in town noticed that he was suddenly reading the Christian Scriptures every day. They concluded that he must have become a Christian! However, Salman was still a Muslim. His reason for reading the Bible was simply that he wanted to learn more about the Christian faith and compare it to Islam.

This gesture by the Christian believers deeply touched him, and he was heartbroken that he had mistreated and persecuted people who loved and even prayed for their enemies!

At Salman's own mosque there was an elderly mullah on duty. The fact that Salman, although considerably younger than he was, had been appointed his superior angered him mightily. Now, his jealousy turned into outright hatred. He spread the rumor everywhere that Salman had apostatized from Islam and had become a Christian.

Salman's parents heard the news. They were livid. Without inquiry, they threw him out of their home. The other mullahs in town issued a fatwa (Islamic court sentence) against him, demanding that he should be hanged. He was not given the opportunity to defend or justify himself. All of a sudden the former persecutor had become the one persecuted. Salman was now homeless and defenseless.

SEARCHING AND FINDING THE TRUTH

Out on the street, with very little money and his life in grave danger, Salman had to ponder what to do next. He decided to visit the leader of the evangelistic team that had given him the New Testament.

When the man recognized Salman, he grew a little nervous.

"Why did you come to me since you hate Christians? Do you intend to beat me up again?" he asked.

"Sir, I have not come to beat you up," Salman replied. "However, the book you gave me has brought me great trouble. My family has put me out on the street and my life is in danger. People think that I have become a Christian. However, I just wanted to find the truth. Do you have the answers to my questions, and can you explain the truth to me?"

The man felt overwhelmed by this situation and referred Salman to a Bible college. Unfortunately, the personnel there also were not able to answer the young, learned mullah's questions to his satisfaction. Additional conversations with various other believers also remained fruitless.

Salman continued to read his New Testament. In the meantime, he had gone to New Delhi, the capital of India. There he met with the pastor of an evangelical church and wanted to discuss with him the questions that burned inside him.

At first, the pastor was skeptical.

"Quite a few Muslims 'with questions' have already come to me as pastor. However, most of them hoped to receive money, or they hoped to gain the favor of some beautiful Christian girl," he said.

Salman explained that he was neither interested in money nor women, but in finding the truth.

The pastor agreed to study the Scriptures with him. He also gave him a couple of evangelistic booklets and introduced him to Mr. Lall, a missionary to Muslims with our organization, Call of Hope.

Together, they studied and discussed the most important dif-
ferences that exist between Islam and Christianity: The Bible af-
firms that Jesus is the Son of God, while Islam vehemently denies
this. The Bible teaches that it is possible to have assurance of
salvation, while in Islam it would be a sin to affirm any certainty
in this regard. Christianity at its core is a message of God's unconditional love for all of mankind, but the Qur'an teaches that
Allah only has regard for the so-called righteous.

At last, Salman knew he had found the answers that he was
searching for. He committed his life to Christ and requested to
be baptized shortly thereafter.

He knew that this constituted the final break from his family
and relatives. He also would never again be able to function and
work as a mullah. But he had decided to follow Jesus, and there
was no turning back.

The Bible teaches us in 2 Corinthians 5:17, "If anyone is in
Christ, he is a new creation. The old has passed away; behold, the
new has come" (ESV).

MISSIONARIES IN KASHMIR

Inwardly, Salman now felt the desire to spread the gospel message among his former Muslim brethren. Just as he had taught
them about what he formerly believed were the truths of Islam,
he now wanted to proclaim the true message of the Bible and the
wonderful news of the love of God in Jesus Christ to all people.

In order to prepare for this task, he joined a Bible college in
1991, from which he graduated four years later. Shortly thereafter,

he married Chandra, a convert from a Hindu background. God blessed the family with the birth of two girls.

Where to go? Brother Salman and Chandra chose probably the most difficult mission field in all of India: the majority-Muslim region of Kashmir in northwestern India.

He knew that this constituted the final break from his family and relatives. But he had decided to follow Jesus, and there was no turning back.

From 1995 until the end of 2011, they served and labored there on behalf of the gospel. In Kashmir, Brother Salman was now doing the very thing that had jump-started his own journey to Christ: traveling throughout the state and handing out gospel tracts and booklets and engaging in conversations with anyone interested to hear more about Jesus.

Meanwhile, Chandra conducted sewing courses for young Muslim girls. These courses not only gave the participants the ability to earn a living for themselves, but also presented an excellent opportunity to communicate the gospel to the girls during the training sessions.

It was not an easy time. Often, the family faced threats and abuse from radical Muslims. False accusations led to summons by the secret police. Rioters armed with iron rods assailed the family. Several times they had to relocate for safety. And still, in the midst of various troubles, they were able to make the gospel known to many Muslims. Over the years, dozens of Muslims accepted Christ as their personal Savior and were baptized.

EXPELLED

This "success" only served to increase the ire of the Muslim community toward Brother Salman and his family.

In 2011, the entire situation exploded. This was the very year the baptism service of former Muslims was secrely filmed and uploaded online. It was the straw that broke the camel's back.

The sharia court took up a case against them. They ordered Salman to appear. He tried to resist the citation, but in the end the threat of abduction issued against his two young girls, Christina and Catherine, weighed more heavily. He had no choice but to comply.

The court logged false and incredible accusations against him. He was accused of bribing Muslims with money to become Christians. Supposedly more than one hundred thousand Muslims had already fallen away from Islam and had become Christians because of his schemes.

The prosecution demanded his immediate arrest and punishment. In the end, the sharia court banned Brother Salman and his wife from ever entering Kashmir again.

It was a very dramatic and traumatic time, especially for the two young girls. Radical Muslims even went as far as hiring assassins to murder the family. The situation became so unsafe that Brother Salman and his family hastily had to flee from Kashmir in November of 2011.

AFFLICTED, BUT NOT DEFEATED

The apostle Paul himself had to go through situations like the one Brother Salman's family experienced. He writes about his experiences in 2 Corinthians 4:8–9 (ESV): "We are afflicted in every way, but not crushed; perplexed, but not driven to despair; persecuted, but not forsaken; struck down, but not destroyed." In all that happened, Brother Salman, his wife, Chandra, and their girls remained sure of the unchanging faithfulness of God in spite of all outward difficulties.

Where to go next? For a period of two years, the family resided in New Delhi. This was also a time of rest, recuperation, and prayer. In 2014, they were ready for a new ministry challenge. They relocated to Lucknow, the city close to Brother Salman's hometown.

At present, the family is still serving the Lord in Uttar Pradesh, Brother Salman's home state. Brother Salman still goes out with Bibles and tracts on the street, seeking to tell Muslims about the love of God for them and win them for Christ.

Sister Chandra still leads sewing courses every year, and many of the young women whom she has taught the art of sewing have made a confession for Christ.

Here, too, the family sometimes faces opposition and hardship because of their work for the gospel. But they know: Whatever happens to them, because the Lord is their Shepherd, they shall never want.

SHOULD WE BE AFRAID OF MUSLIMS?

The experience of Brother Salman's family in Kashmir and his own violent action against Christians when he was still a Muslim remind us of an issue that preoccupies many people in the West:

Should Christians be afraid of Muslim extremists and even Muslims in general?

Three important things should be noted in answer to this question:

First, we have to state the facts. The vast majority of Muslims in the world are peaceful. They wish for peaceful, prosperous lives—for themselves and their families. This is also the main reason behind the increased Muslim immigration to Western countries in recent decades. We should never see Muslims as our enemies. We should see them and meet them as what they are, normal human beings, created and loved by God, and having the same human rights as everyone else.

Second, we have to be realistic. Islam did not have a peaceful beginning, but mainly expanded through conquest. Both the Qur'an and the example of the Prophet Muhammad legitimize the use of force for the spread and enforcement of Islam. This fact is foundational to Islam as a whole. In this respect, Islam cannot be reformed and molded into a "Western," peaceful version, as some hope to do. This is why Western governments should keep a watchful eye on the efforts of Islamic extremism, expansionism, and terrorism in their countries.

Third, the love of God overcomes all fear and hatred. We should neither fear nor hate Muslims and Muslim extremists. Instead, we should pray for them. Jesus Christ died for their sins on the cross, and God's love possesses the power to change their hearts . . . just like He did with Brother Salman.

CHAPTER 10

"I Live in Your Heart"

Sister Jamila
UNITED STATES

THE NEW SHOP ASSISTANT

A couple of times upon entering the fabric shop in Little India, Chicago, Sister Samantha had noticed the new shop assistant. The young woman was shy and sweet and spoke only broken English. Her apparel clearly identified her as Muslim.

She must be from South Asia, Samantha thought. "Who is she?" Samantha asked the shopkeeper.

"Oh—that's Jamila," the shopkeeper replied. "She recently moved here from Bangladesh after her marriage. Her husband lives here. She's still adapting to the new environment. Maybe she could participate in your English language course."

"Well, yes, why not!"

Together, Samantha and the shopkeeper went over to talk to Jamila.

MUSLIMS IN THE WEST

The times are long past when the population of European and North American countries could be characterized as homogeneously "Judeo-Christian." Whereas the traditional "Muslim world" of northern Africa, the Middle East, and far-east Asia continues to be as Muslim as it ever was, Western countries have seen an ever-increasing Muslim population. Currently, Muslims comprise between 5–10 percent of the population of major Western European countries like Germany, France, and Great Britain.[1] The overall Muslim population of all of Europe, currently at about 5 percent, is expected to top 11 percent by 2050.[2] This growth is largely driven by the larger-than-average size of Muslim families, immigration, and the influx of refugees from Muslim-majority countries.

The situation in North America and the United States is similar, although, since there are no Muslim-majority countries in its vicinity, the growth of their Muslim populations is less in comparison to Western Europe. According to some estimates, Muslims currently comprise between 1–2 percent of the population in the US,[3] which is about three to six million people. Many of them are first- or second-generation immigrants. And thousands of new mosques have been built in the last couple of decades.

THE MISSION FIELD RIGHT NEXT DOOR

For Christians, this development has huge implications. In order to reach Muslims for Christ, we don't need to focus exclusively on Muslim-majority countries overseas any more. No, the mission field is right here, right next door. Increasingly, adherents of Islam are our colleagues and neighbors, and they too must be reached with the love of Christ. In whatever small way, every one of us is called to be a missionary to Muslims.

Thankfully, more and more church and ministry initiatives are trying to tackle the task of reaching Muslims in the West with the gospel. One of these ministry initiatives is the South Asian Friendship Center (SAFC) in Chicago. Founded in the mid 1990s by one of the authors of this book, Samuel Naaman, SAFC is located in Chicago's Little India, an ethnically diverse neighborhood where many people from India, Bangladesh, Pakistan, Nepal, and Afghanistan, among others live. Many of them are Muslims. The SAFC's goal is to reach these people for Christ with a loving heart and a helping hand.

JAMILA COMES TO THE CENTER

One way they connect to people from a Muslim background in Little India is through offering free ESL courses (English as a Second Language). This is a great help to those in that community who, coming from an immigrant background and living in a predominantly immigrant community, would otherwise have little opportunity to learn English at all. That is how the SAFC center came into contact with Jamila, the young lady working at the local fabric store.

She had grown up in Bangladesh in a very secure and good Muslim family and was much loved by her parents and siblings. At the age of sixteen, as is customary in her culture, her parents married her off to a young man, Azeem, also a Bangladeshi, who was living in Chicago. After she had turned eighteen, her husband brought her over to the United States.

When Jamila arrived in Chicago, she discovered that her husband Azeem was already living with another woman, and that he had only married her in order to please his parents. Often he would be gone with the other woman for many days on end and leave her at home by herself.

What a shock for a young wife to find out that her husband doesn't really love her and does not even want to be with her! To Jamila, this was worse than the fact that Azeem was already living with a woman. As a Muslim, she was used to the thought that a man could be married to multiple wives. But to be rejected, neglected, and ill-treated by her new husband was devastating to Jamila; and all of this was happening in a foreign country in an unfamiliar environment.

Her mother-in-law, who was living in the same house with her, was controlling. She did not want Jamila's parents to find out about the ill-treatment of their daughter, so she did not allow Jamila to have any kind of communication with her family back home. No phone calls, no letters, nothing.

This is how Jamila came to the center: An introverted, shy, and very, very frightened young woman.

"MUSLIMS ARE GOOD PEOPLE!"

All the staff at the center quickly grew fond of her. Everybody loved Jamila. She was a sweet-natured girl, and to see her suffering, to see her hurt, provoked everyone to kindness and compassion toward her. Her English teacher, Sister Samantha, adopted her like a daughter.

Often, the staff shared about their faith in the Lord Jesus. Jamila listened intently. She would regularly ask for prayer, and the staff would pray for her in the name of Christ. Every time they prayed with her, a sense of peace and comfort overcame Jamila.

The love and care she received at the center had an amazing effect on her. She started to blossom. From underneath the hurt and abuse, the real Jamila started to come out: The shyness disappeared, and she developed into a fun-loving, talkative young woman who wanted to enjoy life.

Whenever the staff shared with her about the Bible, Christianity, or Christ, Jamila would often say in defense, "Well, there are many good Muslims. I was born into a Muslim family, and my mom and dad love each other. Muslims are good people. Maybe that which happened to me—maybe Allah wanted it to happen."

And they wouldn't argue with her.

But Jamila would also say, "I want the peace that you have. I want the inner joy that I can see you have."

"Well, it is available to you!" they said. "But you will have to make a choice, just like we did. The only person who can give you this peace, this joy that will endure in spite of all outward circumstances, is the Lord Jesus. Jamila, Christ loves you, and He died for you so that you don't have to do any good works to try and please Him. His sacrifice and blood already took care of everything.

"Also, Jamila, you don't have to take our word that what we say is the truth. God Himself will show you! You can ask Him, you can test Him, and He will reveal Himself to those who seek Him!"

Jamila listened but wouldn't say anything.

THE VACATION IN BANGLADESH

One day, Jamila arrived at the center, excited and overjoyed. "I am going to Bangladesh!" she exclaimed.

"You are WHAT . . . ?"

"Yes, I am going to Bangladesh! My husband is taking me for a vacation!"

Jamila was so happy.

But right away, Sister Samantha felt uneasy about the matter.

"Jamila, are you sure that there is no trick involved? I mean, you have been married to him for a couple of years already, and he hasn't—so to say—even looked at you! Why should he suddenly want to take you on a vacation?"

Jamila didn't worry too much. She was so very, very excited to go back to her home country, to finally see her parents again, and to have her husband for a while all to herself. So, she didn't question the surprising offer.

"Jamila, just for our peace of mind, bring us your passport, your green card, your flight ticket, and your Social Security card, and we'll take photocopies of it. Just to have them as a backup, in case something happens."

She quickly complied, and a very, very happy Jamila soon left for Bangladesh.

A CALL ON CHRISTMAS EVE

It was almost midnight on Christmas Eve, a couple of weeks after Jamila had left. While Sister Samantha and a friend of hers were visiting and chatting in the living room, the phone rang. Jamila was on the line.

"Jamila!"

"Yes."

"What happened?"

Silence.

Then she said, "My husband has divorced me. He has taken away my passport and my green card and my Social Security card, and he has wiped my bank account empty. He has taken everything, and I am stuck here. But I don't want to stay in this country! I want to come back to the US, I want to make a life for myself!"

Samantha listened and then replied, "Okay, Jamila. We will be praying for you. Let's see what we can do to help you."

Samantha sent the photocopies of Jamila's papers to her in Bangladesh, which they had made before her departure. How grateful she now was that she had made them! With these papers, Jamila went to the American Embassy and explained what had happened to her. She asked for help, so she could return to the United States.

The employee at the embassy who was dealing with her case gave Jamila the runaround. For weeks on end, she was getting nowhere with her request for help. By now, time was starting to count against her. The rules were that if she stayed outside the country for more than six months on end, her US green card would become invalid, and she would have to reapply.

Now, she was already in her fifth month abroad.

JOURNEYING BACK

Sister Samantha called her again one day. "Jamila, we have been praying again for you. Just go back to the embassy one more time and see what happens."

Jamila went. That day she happened to speak directly to the senior immigration officer.

"You know, I have seen you come and go around here. What is your problem?" the officer inquired.

Jamila gave her the whole story and showed her the papers. The immigration officer looked at it, checked some details in the computer system, and then said, "Don't worry."

Then she stamped Jamila's passport. "You can go back."

They booked a flight. Everyone at SAFC celebrated!

Then, two days before her departure, Samantha received a phone call from Jamila.

"I cannot come," she said.

"Why, what happened?"

"My husband has called me from Chicago. He told me that he has filed a complaint with the embassy that I stole jewelry from the house. There now is a registered case against me. As soon as I land in Chicago, the police will come to pick me up and take me to prison."

"Jamila, don't be so foolish. Your ex-husband was just bluffing. He is trying to scare you away from coming back. If there was a case registered against you, it would have shown on the computers at the embassy. There is nothing. Just come!"

She came. She entered the US already a couple of weeks past the allowed six-month period abroad. God held His hand over her, and she didn't encounter any problems at immigration.

THE NIGHT OF THE TWENTY-SEVENTH DAY OF RAMADAN

Since Jamila now had no place to stay, Samantha took her in for a while to stay with her and her family. Here she experienced the love and care of a Christian home firsthand. Thankfully, she also got her former job back at the fabric store without a problem.

Jamila still continued to visit the SAFC center, and everyone loved her. She was still the "baby" of the center.

But something odd happened. When she would try to perform her daily Islamic prayer, she experienced a demonic presence. This scared her immensely, and she stopped reciting her Muslim prayers. Instead, she started to read the Bible, while the staff continued to witness to her about the Christian faith.

It was now the time of Ramadan, the annual Muslim month of fasting. The keeping of Ramadan is one of the five pillars of Islam, and every Muslim is called to strictly observe fasting during the day and is allowed to eat and drink only after sundown. During the month of Ramadan, many Christians worldwide spend extra time in prayer for God to reveal Himself to Muslims for their salvation.

The SAFC staff too devoted extra time to prayer during Ramadan each year. They also would often pray through the night of the twenty-seventh day of Ramadan. To Muslims, this night—the Laylat al-Qadr—is the most holy of all nights of the year, as they believe that during this night Allah revealed the first verses of the Qur'an to Muhammad.

That particular night Sister Samantha and others were conducting a prayer meeting at the Center and pleading with God to intervene in the lives of Muslims. Since Jamila was still a Muslim believer, she naturally did not join in that prayer meeting. Instead, she sat alone back at Samantha's house.

At 10:00 p.m., the phone rang in the center. Jamila was on the line.

"What happened, Jamila?"

"I just accepted the Lord."

"You did WHAT?!"

"I just accepted the Lord."

"Really?"

"Yes."

"That is amazing, Jamila! We are in the middle of a prayer gathering—is there something we can pray for you specifically?" Sister Samantha asked.

"Please pray that I will find the peace that you talk about. And pray that I would grow in the Lord."

At this point, Samantha and the other people praying just started to weep with joy. Not only because Jamila had accepted the Lord Jesus as her personal Savior, but also because of what she had asked for prayer for: She did not ask for money or success, she did not ask for another husband or a child, or for vengeance against her former husband. All she wanted was peace, and to grow to know the Lord more intimately.

"I LIVE IN YOUR HEART!"

That twenty-seventh night of Ramadan became a truly holy night at the center. Rejoicing broke out and praises went up to God for a precious soul that had been saved.

After the prayer meeting had wrapped up, Samantha went home. Jamila was fast asleep.

"Get up, Jamila!"

"What is it?"

"I want to hear what happened; how did you get to accept the Lord!?"

Jamila told the story.

"Do you remember, Samantha, how you told me that I can put Jesus to the test, whether He really is what he claims to be?

"Well, I decided to test him. Reading the Bible, and seeing the peace and joy you have, I really wanted so much to believe in Him. And yet, I felt a pullback, also. I could feel that struggle in me.

"So, while I was lying alone in bed I said, 'Jesus, I am going to put You to the test today. Samantha told me that I can test You. I will stick my hand out off the bed, and You have to physically touch my hand. My teacher told me that You are the King of the universe, so this shouldn't be too difficult for You.'"

Jamila stuck out her hand. Five minutes, ten minutes, fifteen minutes; nothing happened. She pulled her hand back and remained quiet for a couple of minutes. Then she said, "Maybe You didn't hear me; I am going to give You one more chance; please show me that You truly are God."

Again, she stuck out her hand and waited. Nothing happened. She put her hand down again and said, "Father, Son, Holy Spirit, I am giving You one more chance. I have to know that You really are the one true God."

Again, she stuck out her hand: five minutes, ten minutes, fifteen minutes, twenty minutes. Nothing. By now, Jamila was weeping. "Jesus, if I die today and go to hell, it will be Your fault, because I so much wanted to believe in You."

She was tired. As she put down her hand, she laid it on her heart. At that moment, she heard a voice speak to her and say something like, "Jamila, I live in your heart. You have been seeking Me. I have desired you from the beginning of time. You are mine. And I am the God who is pursuing you."

Jamila instinctively knew that this was the voice of God and that Christ was speaking to her. She got up from her bed and got down on her knees, tears streaming down her face. And just as she had been taught how to become a believer by Samantha, she now confessed her sins, gave her heart to the Lord, and made the decision to follow Jesus.

Scripture tells us, "You will seek me and find me when you seek me with all your heart" (Jer. 29:13).

———————

SEIZING OPPORTUNITIES
TO REACH MUSLIMS IN THE WEST

For many centuries, the Muslim world seemed impenetrable to the evangelistic efforts of missionaries. Mission organizations consciously or unconsciously would avoid them: too dangerous, too difficult, too little fruit.

The last several decades have seen a change to this perspective. For the first time in history, Muslims are finding Christ by the hundreds and thousands in countries all over the world! Yet many of those who turn to Christ in Muslim countries continue to suffer persecution, both from the Islamic society around them as well as from a pro-Islamic government that often prohibits Christian conversions.

We, in Western countries, have many wonderful opportunities to reach Muslims living among us. We can freely share the gospel here, uninhibited by government repression. There are no anti-conversion laws; Muslims can freely choose to follow Christ and be baptized without legal punishment. Also, if a Muslim who converts to Christianity in a Western country faces harassment from his or her Muslim relatives, they can be more easily sheltered and protected against violence.

Let's make ample use of the wonderful opportunities that God is giving us to reach all Muslims living around us for Christ!

Epilogue

"Muslims are descendants of Hagar and have been cursed. They excluded themselves from Jesus' salvation": With this argument, many church fathers rejected missional efforts among Muslims over a thousand years ago. Still today, there are renowned "Christian" theologians rejecting mission among Muslims. This time they do so with a humanistic-liberal argument: "Muslims believe in the same, one God, and their religion is Abrahamic, just as Christianity and Judaism." In other words, in former times people said, "Muslims can't be saved"; today they say, "Muslims don't need to be saved."

Even in the worldwide missionary movement, the idea of mission among Muslims was not met with enthusiasm for a long time. A systematic and organized approach to mission among Muslims has only come about in the last century.

Mission work among Muslims is a very risky business. There is no other religion in the world that hates and persecutes the church of Jesus as fanatically as Islam does. Every Muslim learns as a child that Allah has replaced the Christian faith with Islam and the Bible with the Qur'an. Every Muslim child is taught that Jesus is not the Son of God and that He was never crucified. Every Muslim knows: "If I leave Islam and become a Christian, Islam demands the death penalty."

By practical thought, it is indeed not the wisest thing to preach the gospel to Muslims. The enormous theological obstacles in Islam and the sanctions it applies to dissidents make mission work among Muslims seem like an absurd idea to many people.

J. Christy Wilson, who was a well-known missionary in Persia (now Iran), once wrote in the most renowned journal of mission work among Muslims, "The Bible and Moslems," "We can no more apply the truth of the Bible to a Moslem heart than we can raise the dead." This depressing remark is followed by an encouraging conclusion: "Only the Holy Spirit can bring a certain verse or passage into the particular crisis of the individual and make it for him the very Word of God. . . . It is the Word of God, not the word of man, that saves. How necessary, then, that we present the Bible to Moslems under the direction of its real Author—the Holy Spirit. Only He can make it in very fact to them the Word of God for their particular need."[1]

Let us trust that the Lord Himself will touch the hearts of Muslims and enable them to turn to Him. And let us ask the Lord every day to use us also in this endeavor to reach Muslims for Christ!

Notes

INTRODUCTION

1. Neha Sahgal and Besheer Mohammed, "In the US and Western Europe, People Say They Accept Muslims, but Opinions Are Divided on Islam," Pew Research Center, October 8, 2019, https://www.pewresearch.org/fact-tank/2019/10/08/in-the-u-s-and-western-europe-people-say-they-accept-muslims-but-opinions-are-divided-on-islam/.

CHAPTER 1: WHAT A FRIEND WE HAVE IN JESUS

1. "Ghana," The World Factbook, Central Intelligence Agency, last updated January 22, 2021, https://www.cia.gov/the-world-factbook/countries/ghana/.
2. See Sura 33:50.

CHAPTER 2: ONE SENTENCE THAT PIERCED THE HEART

1. "Turkey," The World Factbook, Central Intelligence Agency, last updated January 25, 2021, https://www.cia.gov/the-world-factbook/countries/turkey/.

CHAPTER 3: A "FAKER" BECOMES A TRUE "FOLLOWER"

1. "Christian Persecution," Open Doors USA, 2020, https://www.opendoorsusa .org/christian-persecution/

CHAPTER 4: "JESUS LOVES ME—A WOMAN!"

1. Qur'an 4:34.
2. Q. 2:282.
3. Q. 4:12.

4. Abdullah b. Mahmud al-Mawsili: *Al-Ikhtiyar fi Ta 'lil al-Mukhtar*, vol. III (Lebanon: Dar al-Kutub al-Ilmiyya, 1967), 123; Joseph Schacht, "Talaq," *The Encyclopaedia of Islam*, vol. 9 (Leiden, Netherlands: E. J. Brill, 2000), 151.

CHAPTER 5: THE LADY WHO WANTED TO CLEAN THE CHURCH

1. "Note to Correspondents: Transcript of Press Stakeout by United Nations Special Envoy for Syria, Mr. Staffan de Mistura," United Nations Secretary-General, April 22, 2016, https://www.un.org/sg/en/content/sg/note-correspondents/2016-04-22/note-correspondents-transcript-press-stakeout-united.
2. Qur'an 21:23.
3. Q. 13:27; 14:4; 16:93.
4. Q. 2:15; 7:186.
5. Q. 40:9.

CHAPTER 7: THIRTY-FIVE MILES THROUGH THE BUSH IN ONE NIGHT

1. The Editors of Encyclopedia Britanica, "Johannes Rebmann: German Explorer and Missionary," Britannica, https://www.britannica.com/biography/Johannes-Rebmann.
2. Bukhari, *riqaq* 42; Tirmidhi, *jana 'iz* 8; Ibn Madja, *jana 'iz* 64.

CHAPTER 8: THE LION OF CHRIST

1. Sufism: Islamic mysticism, with a stress on personal piety and mystical experience in the practice of Islam.
2. François Gautier, *Rewriting Indian History* (Delhi, India: India Reseach Press, 1996), 53.
3. Qur'an. 47:19.
4. Q. 3:144.
5. Q. 33:40.
6. Q. 7:157.
7. Q. 19:16–21.
8. Q. 3:49.
9. Q. 5:72; 9:30.
10. Q. 4:48; 5:72.
11. Q. 4:157.

CHAPTER 10: "I LIVE IN YOUR HEART"

1. "Europe's Growing Muslim Population," Pew Research Center, November 29, 2017, https://www.pewforum.org/2017/11/29/europes-growing-muslim-population/.
2. Ibid.
3. Besheer Mohamed, "New Estimates Show U.S. Muslim Population Continues to Grow," Pew Research Center, January 3, 2018, https://www.pewresearch.org/fact-tank/2018/01/03/new-estimates-show-u-s-muslim-population-continues-to-grow/.

EPILOGUE

1. J. Christy Wilson, "The Bible and Moslems," *The Muslim World* 27, no. 3 (July 1937): 239.